Re:CONSIDERING

THE END OF MEN?

Simon Smart

a. Acorn Press

Published by Acorn Press, an imprint of Bible Society
Australia, in partnership with the Centre for Public
Christianity.
ACN 127 775 973
GPO Box 4161
Sydney NSW 2001
Australia
www.publicchristianity.org

© Centre for Public Christianity, 2024. All rights reserved.

ISBN 9780647532959 (pbk)
ISBN 9780647532966 (ebk)

Apart from any fair dealing for the purposes of private
study, research, criticism or review, no part of this work
may be reproduced by electronic or other means without the
permission of the publisher.

Simon Smart asserts his right under section 193 of the
Copyright Act 1968 (Cth) to be identified as the author of
this work.

Scripture quotations are taken from the Holy Bible, New
International Version® Anglicized, NIV® Copyright ©
1979, 1984, 2011 by Biblica, Inc.® Used by permission. All
rights reserved worldwide.

A catalogue record for this
book is available from the
National Library of Australia

Editor: Kristin Argall
Cover and text design: John Healy
Cover image adapted from Doomko / Alamy Stock Vector

About the Centre for Public Christianity

What is the good life?
What does it mean to be human?
Where can I find meaning?
Who can I trust?

In sceptical and polarised times, the Centre for Public Christianity (CPX) seeks to engage the public with a clear, balanced, and surprising picture of the Christian faith. A not-for-profit media company, since 2007 CPX has been joining the dots between contemporary culture and the enduring story of Jesus in the articles, podcasts, books, documentaries, and other resources we produce.

We believe Christianity still has something vital to say about life's biggest questions. Find out more about our team and the work we do at www.publicchristianity.org or follow us on Facebook, Twitter, and Instagram.

About the author

Simon Smart is Executive Director of the Centre for Public Christianity. A former English and History teacher, Simon has a Masters in Christian Studies from Regent College, Vancouver. He was co-presenter and co-writer of the historical documentary *For the Love of God: How the church is better and worse than you ever imagined* and is the host of the *Life & Faith* podcast. Simon's writing has appeared in such places as the ABC, *The Age*, *The Australian*, *The Guardian* and *The Sydney Morning Herald*. He lives on Sydney's northern beaches and is an inept but enthusiastic surfer.

CONTENTS

1. THE DAMAGE DONE 1
A complex story 8

2. WE HAVE A PROBLEM 12
Men and violence 14
The sobering statistics 16
'Locker room talk' 17
Running with the crowd 19
Pornography 20
Wellbeing 21
Confusion setting in 25

3. MODELS OF MASCULINITY 28
Which masculinity? 30
Media and masculinity 31
Early limitations 36
History, politics and masculinity 38
Time to listen 40

4. MEN, MAYHEM AND MUTUAL BENEFIT ... 42
Toxic 44
Broken promises, lost dreams 47
Control 52
Nobody wins unless everybody wins ... 54

5. SIGNS OF LIFE 59
- Evolution 61
- Men making a change 64
- The challenge and reward of honesty and openness 66
- Changing our definitions 68
- Positive visions 72

6. REMEDIES 75
- The river of knowledge 76
- Community and building the village 78
- Structure and personal responsibility 82
- Calculated risk 85
- Rites of passage 87
- Positive peer pressure 89
- HEAL jobs 90
- Restitution and recovery 91

7. ANCIENT WISDOM FOR MODERN TIMES 94
- Love as a framework 94
- Authority and vulnerability 97
- An old story for a new day 99
- A radical life 100
- Refusing to walk on by 102
- Jesus and women 106
- A modern code? 108

NOTES 116

Re:CONSIDERING

1. THE DAMAGE DONE

I sometimes wonder what happened to Ratty Gardener – or the Rat, as most people knew him. Every single day of his school life, Ratty would ride the packed school bus from wherever he lived to the agricultural boys' high school that we both attended on the outskirts of the large regional town where I lived. No matter how uncomfortably full that bus got on the thirty-minute ride back to town, the aisle jammed with sweaty, swaying kids, there was always one seat spare. The mob had decided nothing could be worse than sitting next to the silent, miserable lump of a kid with green teeth and Coke bottle glasses. He would sit alone, impassive, staring out the window. Who knows what he could have been thinking?

Or what about Chomper? He was a mouthy, blond, surfy kid from the coast, whose mistake was to stand out from his rural counterparts. One boy took it upon himself to form the anti-Chomper association and collected a bunch of supporters who committed themselves to making Chomper's life hell each day. He didn't last beyond Year 8.

It was a brutal environment. Boarders, mostly from farms in the north-west of New South Wales, made up the bulk of the school population. From the age of 12, they lived in big, open dormitories with wooden floors, no heating – despite bitterly cold winters – and only a bed and a locker for any kind of personal space.

Left in the 'care' of a Year 12 boy, these kids were subject to noxious rituals of arbitrary 'discipline'. Occasionally they'd be bent over beds and hit with brooms, or terrorised on Saturday nights when drunk 'prefects' (everyone was a prefect in their final year) would come back at midnight and get their kicks from having small boys stand at attention next to their bed, terrified, while a mock military inspection of their area took place. Always the threat of violence permeated the air. One noncompliant boy I knew was blindfolded while a stock whip was cracked around his head. Another was held out of the window of a three-storey building by his ankles.

Teachers were nowhere to be seen. More than just turning a blind eye, they encouraged a system of rough justice handed out by senior students not mature enough to know better. Those boys had, of course, been subject to the same environment all their schooling careers. Unsurprisingly, they

1. The Damage Done

simply acted out what they'd been shown and were never shown anything different.

The bullying was so systemic that it was barely noticed. The seniority system, which demanded obedience from anyone younger than you, occasionally got out of hand, but the attitude was hey, you have to expect some collateral damage in these situations.

Looking back, I now know I was immersed in an environment that was unrelentingly racist, misogynist, homophobic and anti-intellectual. The picture of masculinity that I absorbed was narrow, monocultured and cruel.

And I loved it.

I was proud of my school. I'd inherited from my older brothers a romanticised perspective on the place. I imagined it was superior to the other schools in town. I thought the uniform symbolised something special and I wore it proudly – embarrassingly so when I think back to that. I'd been encouraged to appreciate the heritage that comes from decades of excelling at footy and cricket, and a brotherly love born out of torrid survival. I was very much part of the system and did nothing to subvert or challenge it.

And it wasn't all bad. It would be disingenuous of me to present it like that. There were good guys there – students and staff. Some of them are still friends of mine over thirty years later. There was camaraderie, black humour; some very funny moments. I happened to love sport and for that, I was considered part of the in-crowd. (Or at least not on the outer.) I loved the sense of being part of something substantial. It was a way of being that really did offer an identity to those who managed to fit the mould. The truth is I didn't know any better and had nothing to compare it with.

But I now know grown men irreparably damaged by the experience, so even my positive memories of the place are tarnished by that.

These days David Hastie is an Associate Professor of Education. But from the age of 12, he spent nearly two years as a boarder at my high school and it had a lifelong impact on him. Recently we connected, and it was sobering to hear about his experiences. 'I suspect many of the boys from that boarding house have faced the challenge of living with a form of PTSD throughout their adult life, and I regret to say I am no exception,' he told me.

> It was, frankly, like living on the island of the Lord of the Flies, except that the adults were actually on that island, and doing nothing. The adults, and their structures, had utterly failed us. Putting such unchecked power into the hands of children

was always going to lead to emphasising the worst parts of their humanity, and the empowering of the very worst amongst them. I suppose, had I stayed at that school, that I myself would have made the natural transition from victim to perpetrator.

An atmosphere of crippling fear and the threat of violence, that 'loomed like a dark cloud over all of us', matches my memories of the place, especially for the boarders. When I asked him whether he had any positive memories of the experience, I found his answer to be full of pathos:

> I have a positive memory of roaming around with a small group of friends unencumbered on the weekends. The boys were completely unsupervised. We used to go down to the wild banks of the … river, away from the violence and threats in the dorm areas, and just play, making mudslides and building bows and arrows and cubbies out of reeds. We were just kids.

Hastie agrees with me in thinking that with the right leadership, what could have been done in that environment to generate a healthy culture doesn't bear thinking about. You wouldn't have had to lose any of the great sporting opportunities, or the commitment to pushing physical limits, to create an entirely different atmosphere. One where a love of learning would be fostered and celebrated; a passion for literature, music, drama and art would be encouraged; and different versions of what it is to be a boy would be celebrated, not crushed. It could even be a place where it was a point of pride to support and protect the weak, rather than devise new and creative ways to hurt them. It's easy for me now to see how you could cultivate a school culture where the education of the whole person – mind, body and spirit – would be considered worthwhile.

When Australian writer Tim Winton wrote his novel *The Shepherd's Hut*, about the life of Jaxie Clackton, a neglected, abused teenaged boy on the run, he drew on his sense of a particularly Australian version of masculinity gone wrong. Winton is himself anything but a judgemental observer of human behaviour. He is deeply sympathetic to his flawed characters, but he also writes out of a frustration with the models of being a man that we sometimes limit ourselves with.

When I interviewed Winton about that novel, he had this to say about the kind of culture Jaxie was born into:

> I'm interested in the way that men are blind to how rotten patriarchy and misogyny is *for them* as well. … You watch these lovely, tender, vulnerable, graceful boys, having all those lovely qualities – which are natural qualities in boys as

1. The Damage Done

> much as in girls – having them shamed or beaten out of them, so that they cleave to one very narrow view of masculinity, which is hard, narrow, silent, angry, and taking, never giving. It impoverishes kids, it impoverishes boys, it impoverishes their manhood, and endangers everybody around them – and it's not necessary.[1]

For Winton, there is so much more that can be on offer for young people as they navigate their way towards adulthood, and he cites the typical rites of passage of young Australians as withering and restrictive. Winton is probably reflecting on what he has observed listening to conversations between young men while waiting for a wave in the surf. Perhaps that's a particular culture. But anyone who has found themselves exhaling a resigned sigh at the sound of yet another full-throated rendition of 'Here's to Robbo, he's true blue …' as the obligatory preparation for skolling a beer will understand what he means in being able to imagine a more expansive and enriching culture.

Times have changed significantly since I was at school in the 1980s. (I can't imagine my old school could be run anything like it was back then.) And our country has matured and grown. We are more comfortable with difference than we were. We are at least beginning to wrestle with the shameful statistics on Indigenous wellbeing and the stain and trauma of the past for our First Nations peoples. We have made massive leaps in terms of the opportunities that exist for women and girls. The vicious homophobia that was commonplace when I was young is no longer socially acceptable. Our imaginations have expanded in terms of what it means to be a man, and there are more answers to that question than when I was young.

But in each of these areas there is a long way to go. (In some of them we've barely begun.) The #MeToo movement unearthed shocking experiences of women at the hands of predatory and powerful men. Domestic violence remains a horrific and seemingly intractable issue and overwhelmingly, males are the ones dishing out the violence.

A complex story

We live in an age of binaries, a world in which we all too often view others through our own black-and-white lens. In some circles, the idea of the 'male' represents everything that is regressive and offensive.

1. The Damage Done

The problem is, most men and boys do not neatly fit into an easily defined category. It's way too simplistic to label all masculinity toxic without addressing the nuances and various shades of this story. It's important to remember that wherever there exists negative male behaviour, boys and young men are subject to it as well. In some cases, it's all they've known.

The other side of this 'male dilemma' coin is that there are strong signs that many men are struggling. Suicide rates for men are truly alarming. Boys fall behind girls in academic performance, and confusion amongst boys about what it might mean to be 'a good man' clouds the horizon of hopeful futures and possibilities. I'll address these issues early on.

This little book is an attempt to provoke a healthy conversation about positive masculinity, including finding ways to foster environments that help rather than hinder the development of boys and men. While my focus is on the condition of boys and men, this of course has enormous implications for women and girls. I have a young adult son and daughter, and my interest in this subject has grown in no small part because of how I think about their lives and that of their friends who are also special to me.

I have an old friend who had a brief but deeply unpleasant experience as a boarder at my school the year before I arrived there. It's no surprise he didn't make it beyond Year 7 before heading back to the coastal town he came from. He has remained an unfailingly kind, thoughtful, sensitive bloke with a deep interest in justice for the marginalised and oppressed. These were not qualities that set you up for acceptance at my school, and while he has kicked on to do good things in his life, he carries deep scars that he would admit have not entirely left him. There must be many others with similar wounds.

I guess it's in thinking about my friend, and others like him, and also experiencing environments that contrast so vividly with the one that I grew up in, that I have come to care so much about this subject.

I'm aware of the danger of wading into an area of such controversy, especially in such a short book where it will be impossible to deal in sufficient depth with all the issues discussed. Raised eyebrows have met me whenever I have mentioned this project to friends. Given that I am a white, middle-aged, heterosexual man, there will be some who feel me immediately disqualified from the discussion. But I think this is an everyone conversation.

1. The Damage Done

As will be more than obvious, this is not an attempt to wrestle with gender theory, for instance, or to make definitive statements about current discussions regarding gender mutability. But it is an honest response to my own experiences, hunches and hopes, and an attempt to consider how we can do things better and in a way that serves our whole community.

I do believe that personal growth involves the interplay between physical, emotional and spiritual needs, and that we miss something vital when the spiritual is left out of the picture. My own faith tradition is Christian, and that informs and undergirds the way I perceive many of the issues raised here. But I don't believe you would have to share my faith to be part of this conversation in the way I have framed it.

I have a deeply held belief that with the right guidance from older men worth emulating, most boys will thrive and become the best version of themselves. They'll then be in a better position to be partners and fathers. Everyone benefits. I've seen it happen. There is so much good to be done in offering a positive and life-giving vision that young people can live into, and I'm very much of the view that such a dynamic is possible, even in these days of growing polarisation, cynicism and fear.

Re:CONSIDERING

2. WE HAVE A PROBLEM

On a Sunday morning in August 2020, Chantelle Doyle and her husband Mark Rapley were surfing at Port Macquarie's Shelley Beach on the New South Wales mid-north coast when she was attacked by a juvenile great white shark estimated to be 10 foot in length. These kinds of attacks are rare and impossible to predict. Surfers know the risks of being in the ocean and in the domain of these large killers, but they are typically willing to bank on the stats being in their favour. Doyle, an environmental scientist, no doubt had that approach, but her number did come up and to her horror she found herself that morning in the jaws of the dreaded monster of the seas.

Her husband, realising what was happening, immediately paddled to where she was, jumped off his board and began punching the shark hard and repeatedly. Eventually it let go and swam away. He and other rescuers managed to get Chantelle to shore. She was airlifted to hospital with serious

2. We Have a Problem

lacerations to her right leg, but she survived to tell the tale.

'I did what anyone would have done,' Rapley said when in front of the TV cameras. Others of us watching the news bulletins were left to wonder, if faced with the same situation, whether we would in fact act quite like he did. We also had to admit that we hoped never to find out!

Six months before this moment of laudable bravery, a very different story took place in the eastern suburbs of Brisbane. On the morning of 19 February 2020, Hannah Clarke and her three small children aged six, four and three were in their car on a school drop-off run when her estranged husband and father of the children attacked the family. Dousing the interior of the car in petrol, he set it alight. He then prevented a bystander from offering assistance before killing himself with a knife. All three children died at the scene, and Hannah Clarke, severely burned, passed away in hospital later that day. Hannah Clarke had taken out a Domestic Violence Order against her husband, but as is too often the case, the court-issued protection document meant nothing to him in his destructive rage.

These two stories, polar opposites and extreme in nature, are illustrative of vastly different examples of men deploying their physical

Men and violence

I have always had a horrid fascination with the violence of men. And I have witnessed my fair share of it. I remember a night when I was at university, waiting with two other friends for a cab back to our college, when the doors of the pub across the road burst open and two enormous brawling men emerged throwing wild punches at each other. Two or three bouncers tried but failed to contain them, and a woman who was presumably a friend of one of them got tangled up in the chaos and fell to the ground. But nothing could stop what was a really vicious assault that went on and on until finally one of the combatants succumbed to the blows and finished up bleeding and senseless on the pavement.

Back in the days when the Sydney Cricket Ground Hill existed, I experienced some incredible day/night cricket matches as a spectator on that famed mound of grass. Hours into drinking sprees, shirtless, sunburnt, drunken men would be sufficiently offended by another patron to 'go the biff'. This was much to the delight of those around them, who would offer a rousing ovation as the offenders punched on and were inevitably led away to the paddy wagons waiting outside the ground. It was amazing how often this happened; it was just part of the experience in those days. There was a sense of theatre to it all, but again, I was often shocked at the savageness on display.

I love all sports, and growing up I was especially taken with rugby league. I still am. In the 70s and 80s this already violent sport was unbelievably tough. A friend of mine recently described modern-day footy as like a polite dinner party conversation by comparison. If you ever watch highlights of a game from that era, it is astonishing how brutal it was. Intimidation, dominance, fighting and trying to maim your opponent with fists, elbows or knees came with the territory.

I didn't get to play much rugby league. I would have loved to. I had some skills. I could catch, kick and pass pretty well. But my aspirations were thwarted by my parents recognising that I was not big enough, strong enough, fast enough or, let's be honest, tough enough. When I did get to play a little bit at university, I remember being blown away by the ferocity of the physical contact. But the feeling of being in a battle together with your mates was intoxicating.

I even grew up enjoying watching boxing. Heavyweight contests like Muhammad Ali's battles with George Foreman or Joe Frazier were epic and remain the stuff of sporting folklore. I defy anyone not to be captivated by the drama and brutal artistry of a Sugar Ray Leonard vs Marvelous Marvin Hagler bout. The skill mixed with astonishing courage, tenacity and physical and mental resolve captivated my young mind.

In short, as a young guy I found the violence of men, depending on the context, both disturbing and exhilarating.

The context is crucial of course.

The sobering statistics

The reality is that the relationship between men and violence continues to be problematic. In the years since Hannah Clarke and her children lost their lives in such appalling circumstances, the stats have ground on relentlessly with an average of one woman in Australia losing her life at the hands of an intimate partner every week. Family violence and/or intimate partner violence is the leading cause of serious injury, disability and death for women. One in three women have experienced physical or sexual violence, or both, perpetrated by a man they know.[1] Around 95% of all victims of violence, whether women or men, experience that violence at the hands of a male.[2]

A study released in 2021 found that if a woman earns more than her male partner, her chances of being a victim of domestic violence increase by 35%.[3] Clearly some men struggle to handle situations that deviate from the traditional breadwinner role, which doesn't say much for their fragile egos.

'Locker room talk'

White Ribbon Australia – a social movement aimed at eliminating gendered violence – believes that attitudes towards women sit on a continuum that might begin with sexist jokes but then extend to things much more serious. The logic is that the atmosphere that allows those seemingly 'harmless' things to occur also contributes to an environment of social attitudes, behaviours and systems that are detrimental to the place of women and girls.

When even the prospective president of the United States can be heard to joke about 'grabbing p_ _ _ y' and that not be considered a bridge too far, it's clear that demeaning talk about women, while perhaps less prevalent than it once was, remains a common reality.

When I was backpacking around the world in the mid-90s, I found myself on a bus between Istanbul and Çanakkale in Türkiye. I was on a well-worn path to Anzac Cove and other fabled battle sights of the Gallipoli peninsula. On that bus was a group of young Australian men making the pilgrimage that so many do from their temporary bases in various parts of Europe and the UK. They were large, intimidating and aggressive. Boisterous, rude and patronising to the locals, they quickly mistook me for an ally and proceeded to loudly boast of exploits that were at best anti-social and in some cases pretty much criminal.

I put on headphones and pretended not to be able to hear their vile stories of intimidating and mistreating anyone unfortunate enough to be in their path. There was a violence to their talk and an unmistakable sexual aggressiveness. It was a display of the worst version of men out and about and unrestrained by any moral sensibility or accountability. Is it just the way things are?

2. We Have a Problem

Running with the crowd

In February 2020, ABC TV's *Four Corners* program featured elite Melbourne boys' school St Kevin's College, Toorak. On show, at least according to the story as presented, was a culture characterised by entitlement, closed-shop loyalty and aggressive sexism. Footage of a crowd of St Kevin's boys on a public tram chanting crude and sexist songs, oblivious to or unconcerned about the public perception of their behaviour, suggested deep inculturation. Ex-students were interviewed and gave accounts of an exhilarating atmosphere of bravado and strength when all the boys were together, but the same dynamic leading to deeply regrettable outcomes as well.

Ex-Melbourne Girls' College student Eartha Hewett was very familiar with that culture and its weaknesses. 'I think that these people are really kind and loving and sweet when they're by themselves, but then they're surrounded by their mates and you're all doing, I guess, you know, silly stuff, and all your friends are like, "oh boys will be boys. This is what we do". It's like, no. This behaviour is wrong. It's not "boys will be boys". It's not anything like that. It's not OK,' she said.[4]

Former student Luke Macaronas admits to having sung the same chants that were captured on film and caused such controversy. Being caught up in the crowd clearly has an impact on otherwise decent and respectful boys (as well as cruel and disrespectful boys). The pressure to conform is powerful. 'Every guy knows the hot shame of being surrounded by his mates and looking weak or looking stupid. That is … the main force that is driving this kind of behaviour … everyone falls into line, because that's what you're expected to do,' Macaronas explained.[5] The result in these contexts can be, and often is, truly deplorable behaviour.

It's clear that the nature and character of the crowd you walk in is extremely influential – a reality not restricted to elite boys' schools.

Pornography

Pornography is an especially modern problem, and it amazes me that more people don't talk about it as such. When I was a teenager, people had to work hard to get access to porn. Occasionally someone on the school bus would have a magazine that was passed around to wide-eyed amazement. These days, the pervasiveness of the internet means that it takes a conscious effort to avoid pornography, and it's much more socially acceptable. According to the website of activist group Collective Shout, more than 60% of girls and more than 90% of boys have seen online porn.[6] And that porn presents powerful messages about men, women, sex and power. Some of the statistics are alarming, especially relating to the eroticisation of violence against women. In popular pornography, 88% of scenes include acts of physical aggression like gagging, choking and slapping, and 48% of scenes contain verbal aggression.[7] The distorted view of sex and relationships presented by a medium that in some cases forms the main sex education for young people is surely a concern. It's something that needs addressing with sober, open conversations that draw out the implications of this kind of 'education'.

Wellbeing

An examination of some of the worst statistics and traits of negative male behaviour can easily turn into simplistic and unhelpful generalisations or condemnations regarding half the population. The truth is there are worrying signs that boys and men are not doing well on a whole host of important measurements.

In education, boys are struggling to keep up with their female peers, especially at school ages and stages. Even allowing for the obvious difference in maturity levels, it's surely a concern that boys have consistently poorer outcomes than girls when it comes to national literacy standards. More boys leave school early than girls do. They study a narrower range of subjects and have lower scores than girls, and fewer go on to higher education. These kinds of results are found not only in Australia but also in New Zealand, the United States and the United Kingdom.[8] In school, 90% of children with behavioural problems are boys[9] and 85% of children with learning problems are too. Worldwide, boys are 50% more likely than girls to be below basic proficiency in reading, science and maths.[10] Further, a large study out of the UK suggests that boys' IQs have dropped by 15 points since the 1980s.[11]

Marleen De Bolle, lead author of a major study into sex differences in personality traits among adolescents across cultures, writes about the consequences of differing rates of maturity and development:

> Our findings demonstrate that adolescent girls consistently score higher than boys on personality traits that are found to facilitate academic achievement, at least within the current school climate. Stated differently, the current school environment or climate might be in general more attuned to feminine-typed personalities, which make it – in general – easier for girls to achieve better grades at school.[12]

In a 2020 article, 'Educational Gender Gaps', Shelly Lundberg from the University of California makes the case that educational goals and performance are heavily associated with social and cultural forces linked to gender identity:

> A peer-driven search for masculine identity drives some boys toward risk-taking and noncompliance with school demands that hampers school achievement, relative to girls. Aspirations are linked to social identities – what you want and expect depends on who you think you are – and profound differences in the norms defining masculinity and femininity create a gender gap in educational trajectories.[13]

Lundberg believes that when masculinity is conceived as a 'precarious state' that requires 'continual proof and validation', it further stifles boys' already faltering educational advancement.

Writing for *The Atlantic*, Hannah Rosin asks whether we are approaching a tipping point where modern economies are most suited to women, leaving boys in an unstable position. 'The post-industrial economy is indifferent to men's size and strength,' she writes. 'The attributes that are most valuable today – social intelligence, open communication, the ability to sit still and focus – are, at a minimum, not predominantly male. In fact, the opposite may be true.'[14] Rosin, writing in 2010, said of the 15 job categories projected to grow in the following decade in the US, all but two were occupied mostly by women.[15]

Health outcomes generally do not reflect a happy picture either. In Australia, men die six years younger on average than women – at 79 versus 85; men are more likely to die by cancer than women, particularly from bowel, lung and liver cancer; and men account for more than 90 per cent of workplace deaths.[16] Around one-quarter of boys and men in Australia, Britain, Canada, Germany, Poland and Spain are obese.[17]

But it's the mental health stats that might be the most alarming. Government figures released in 2020 revealed a record-breaking 2502 male suicides (816 were females). Of the nine daily suicides in Australia, seven will be male. A 2014/15 study found that around 1 in 4 (23%) males aged 16–24 years had experienced symptoms of a mental disorder.[18]

2. We Have a Problem

Confusion setting in

The stereotypical male unable to articulate his feelings is a well-worn trope, but it has some substance. It's surely less of an issue than when I was young, but it remains a challenge with significant implications. American philosopher Martha Nussbaum, reflecting on recent psychological literature, suggests that large numbers of boys, schooled as they are to be ashamed of their feelings, suppress important emotions:

> When they are frightened, they don't know how to say it … Often they turn their own fear into aggression. Often, too, this lack of a rich inner life catapults them into depression in later life. We are all going to encounter illness, loss, and ageing, and we're not well prepared for these inevitable events by a culture that directs us to think of externals only, and to measure ourselves in terms of our possessions of externals.[19]

Since at least the 1950s, masculine identity has undergone change and adjustment to a vastly different world, and that adjustment has not always been easy. In 2019, the American Psychological Association (APA) designated 'traditional masculinity' – marked by stoicism, competitiveness, dominance and aggression –

as harmful. The description of what that meant included anti-femininity, achievement-focus, resisting the appearance of weakness, and a disposition towards adventure, risk and violence. Various commentators have voiced the reasonable objection that the APA makes no mention of the ways in which some of these characteristics could, in the right context, be thought of as positive and be deployed in beneficial directions.[20]

Men and boys have been caught between a traditional picture of the ideal male as independent, risk-taking, aggressive, heterosexual and rational – which has not entirely left us – and society's growing idealisation of nurture, emotional expression and other traits more typically considered feminine. Reflecting on this modern dilemma, William R. Fuller writes:

> The altering of the masculine formula, learned and ingrained through institutions, media, and peer and parental feedback, leaves many modern men in conflict between traditional patriarchal hegemonic masculinity (machismo) and the not yet defined (but increasingly culturally promoted) new masculinity.[21]

What does it mean to be a good man today – a healthy, well-adjusted man who adds to his community and thrives as an individual? How do we go about creating spaces that increase the likelihood of boys growing into men you'd want to be around if you were a child, a teenager, a woman, or another man? What are the lessons, the rituals, the wisdom that can be imparted to foster an environment where boys can become their best selves and be a gift to those around them? These are the questions I am interested in pursuing.

Re:CONSIDERING

3. MODELS OF MASCULINITY

The Secret Life of Walter Mitty, the much-loved 2013 film adaptation of James Thurber's short story from 1939, is a favourite of our family. We've watched it together more times than any other movie. A central character, who haunts the story and yet is mostly conspicuous by his absence, is Sean O'Connell, perfectly played by Sean Penn.

A photojournalist of legendary status, O'Connell has captured some of the most dramatic images in the storied history of *LIFE* magazine. Everything about him oozes a masculine heroic aura. He's ridiculously hardcore, popping up only in the most dangerous and forbidding places. He is unknowable, shrouded in mystery. A distant loner in total control, whether dodging bullets in a war zone, strapped to the top of a biplane flying into the heart of an erupting volcano while everyone else flees, or sitting in solitary, zen-like concentration on a remote alpine peak waiting to snap a shot of the elusive snow leopard.

3. Models of Masculinity

O'Connell is himself impossibly hard to pin down but ever reliable in coming up with the creative goods. His photographic negatives that arrive at *LIFE* HQ are met with breathless anticipation. The film roll will often be bloodstained! He's of no fixed address and only communicates through mail sent from obscure and exotic places. While the rest of us live our lives of comparative staid convention, O'Connell operates on a rugged, romantic and adventurous plane. Weathered and tanned, he's truly at home only in the wild.

It's a parody of course, and a very funny one. Sean O'Connell is one of my favourite characters. But his place in this story is illustrative of something that is worth thinking about in our consideration of masculinity: the way various forms of media portray ideal manhood means that men and boys are presented with a conflicted and confusing picture of how they should aim to be. This is especially the case in light of the huge social shifts that have occurred in the last forty years.

Which masculinity?

Boys and young men today may well be left wondering about which version of masculinity they are supposed to aspire to. It's not at all clear what that should be, and the confusion presents a particularly modern challenge. Are they to aim for the traditional protector/provider? The Renaissance man? The empathetic creative? The sports jock? The warrior? The outdoor expert for every occasion? The reliable, practical, home-renovating type? The free-spirited wanderer? The genius geek on the road to tech-driven wealth? The list could go on of course.

The films and TV shows I consumed as a child were from a simpler age of goodies and baddies and, I must admit, stories that mostly involved the spectacle of men carrying out violent retribution for evils committed by various miscreants. Everything from *Batman* to the *Six Million Dollar Man* and, when I was older, Clint Eastwood or Charles Bronson, offered up rudimentary narratives that involved a clear notion of the ideal man for a crisis. But it was all very limiting. The world has changed enormously in that regard, creating a richer, more complex, multilayered image of what it might look like to be a man today.

And yet the smorgasbord of messages that boys are bombarded with from the proliferation of media they are exposed to today creates a bewildering environment to navigate, with frequently contradictory messages of what men are supposed to be. There has been a rejection of traditional masculine traits in the wake of much-needed feminist progress, while at the same time many of those older characteristics are stubbornly present in the deep-rooted narratives that shape our collective consciousness.

Media and masculinity

Author Mark Moss investigates the impact of all forms of media on men's understanding of masculinity. He finds that, where once there was a relatively simple set of templates to follow – largely limited to business, sport and government – today a huge variety of competing 'masculinities' now vie for legitimacy. Men will, he says, typically select one or, more often, a combination of different elements to construct a version of themselves that will work, and that fluctuates depending on the influence of media, culture and society, and the context they find themselves in.[1]

It has always been the case that acceptable templates of masculinity are largely socially constructed and often extremely limiting. They are composed of archetypes and media fabrications that profoundly impact how males think about themselves and judge themselves in relation to others. Roles that men aspire to are often completely unattainable, but that doesn't stop them from basing their behaviour and aspirations on these models.[2]

Findings in the field of men's studies suggest that there are a group of masculine traits that have been around for centuries, and despite large-scale social shifts in recent decades, they have not changed much. This is the case in at least four key ways: to be masculine means not being effeminate; embracing an ethic of competition; being detached and 'cool'; and finally, exhibiting a tendency towards risk-taking.[3]

While not as rigid as they once were, these characteristics remain something to measure yourself against. Think Daniel Craig's version of James Bond. He embodies all of these traits *and* adds the ability to seduce and to kill, combined with a suave, stylish sensibility and, in later films, even a vulnerable and sensitive side.

3. Models of Masculinity

Moss identifies a series of archetypes present in media of many forms, including not only film and television, but also video games, marketing and advertising that promote more traditional masculine characteristics. Even when these archetypes no longer have much real-world application, they persist as symbols and iconic representations in the male imagination. These archetypes include:

- the cowboy
- the big-game hunter
- the warrior/soldier
- the explorer/adventurer.

Tapping into these images are marketers for motorcycles, hardware stores and camping supplies. Ads for off-road vehicles – largely bought by city-dwelling office workers yearning for escape from urban life – appeal to latent masculine ideals from earlier eras. For example, Moss describes Jack Daniel's bourbon as the symbol of 'rebel manhood, frontier individuality, and … the gunfighter mystique'.[4] Sipping a couple of JDs and Coke in the corner of a suburban pub on a Friday night might not measure up to the mystique, but that's the way the illusion of advertising works.

Interestingly, each of Moss' archetypes contain echoes of violence. Moss suggests that young males today receive incompatible and contradictory messages: be masculine and celebrate traditional masculine traits, yet also rein yourself in and respect what society now considers appropriate.[5] We might think of rugby league players today who are paid to be recklessly violent in their careers. That's what we love about them. They are the modern equivalent of the gladiators in the Roman arena. Yet unlike their ancient counterparts, they are also expected to be virtuous role models for kids once they are off the field. That rarely goes well. But it remains the case that aggressiveness is admired and celebrated on the sports field, in the boardroom, perhaps even on the playground. Together, these mixed messages create a paralysing confusion.

Psychologists Dan Kindlon and Michael Thompson make a similar point to Moss. They say that on TV and in film and video games, the images of masculinity that are offered are of impossibly powerful supermen. In advertising, men are tough, drive trucks and drink beer (or perhaps cider!). And noticeably these days, even on the occasions when these stereotypes are subverted, the male becomes a figure of fun or buffoonery set against the competent and eye-rolling female. Kindlon and Thompson see a seriousness to all this, noting the damaging rituals that boys feel compelled to live out, often centred around their experiences of heavy drinking, fighting, casual sex and passing out: 'Our culture coopts some of the most impressive qualities a boy can possess – their physical energy, boldness, curiosity, and action orientation – and distorts them into a punishing, dangerous definition of masculinity.'[6]

Feminist writer Susan Faludi laments the way in which, by the dawn of the 21st century, 'ornamental culture'– where decorative or consumer roles replace serious engagement in public life – had managed to trap men in the same manner it had trapped women for so long. The consumer world of movies, sport, music videos and magazines promulgates a message of manhood as a performance game to be won in the marketplace.

> In a culture of ornament ... manhood is defined by appearance, by youth, and attractiveness, by money and aggression, by posture and swagger, and 'props,' by the curled lip and petulant sulk and flexed biceps, by the glamour of the cover boy, and by the market-bartered 'individuality' that sets one astronaut or athlete or gangster above another.[7]

The contrast to a previous era in which men had a clear purpose, responsibility, and sense of duty to the good of others is stark, and Faludi believes the loss associated with that shift has been profound.

Early limitations

The narrowing of the vision of what it is to be a male starts in childhood, and not only on the screen. As the mother of three young boys, author Ruth Whippman laments the narratives they are exposed to at an early age, which she says, in her boys' experience, are almost all limited to two men in combat – one victorious, the other brutally defeated. Writing for *The New York Times*, Whippman argues that even the fictional worlds of small girls reflect a much wider, richer, more complex emotional range than the boys in their classes. Whereas little girls will be exposed to stories framed around people, friendships, emotions, internal dramas and also the competing emotional needs of others, boys encounter narrative worlds of 'almost zero emotional complexity – no interiority, no negotiating or nurturing or friendship dilemmas or internal conflict. None of the mess of being a real human in constant relationship with other humans.'[8]

Even if Whippman is overstating that dynamic (and she might be), where it exists, such an imbalance feeds an early lack that, as she says, can have long-term implications, impacting the

3. Models of Masculinity

learning of skills required to develop a healthy moral, psychological and emotional life:

> The lack of positive people-focused stories for boys has consequences for them and girls. In the narratives they consume, as well as the broader cultural landscape in which they operate, girls get a huge head start on relational skills, in the day-to-day thorniness and complexity of emotional life. Story by story, girls are getting the message that other people's feelings are their concern and their responsibility. Boys are learning that these things have nothing to do with them.[9]

Comedian Michael Black agrees. 'To be a girl today is to be the beneficiary of decades of conversation about the complexities of womanhood, its many forms and expressions,' he writes.[10] That there are few similar resources for boys has left them stuck in a suffocating, outdated notion of manhood, without a language to express their feelings about this predicament:

> Men feel isolated, confused and conflicted about their natures. Many feel that the very qualities that used to define them – their strength, aggression and competitiveness – are no longer wanted or needed; many others never felt strong or aggressive or competitive to begin with. We don't know how to be, and we're terrified.[11]

Help may be on the way. There are plenty of examples of recent films and streaming series that offer up storylines and characters expressing a full range of male emotion. Mr Rogers, played by Tom Hanks in *A Beautiful Day in the Neighborhood*, imaged the ideal 'father' – embodying a self-assured strength combined with kindness, emotional insight and heart-melting gentleness. Apple TV's Ted Lasso, the hokey and extremely unconventional football coach, for all his buffoonery and determined optimism, carries off an engaging portrait of someone inspiring young, selfish men to be the best version of themselves they can be.

These kinds of offerings suggest that men want and need greater life goals, self-awareness and deeper personal relationships. But as movie reviewer Manohla Dargis reminds us, 'For all the male introspection, though, our movies still love heroic and villainous men, spirited and supportive ladies – the majority white – along with simple moralizing and tidy, exultant endings.'[12]

History, politics and masculinity

Different periods of history present different challenges for what it means to be a man and what characteristics are deemed desirable.

3. Models of Masculinity

Several commentators make reference to a shift in politics and pop culture after the 9/11 terrorist attacks on the United States. Once again, we witnessed an emphasis on the rugged, heroic protector, as well as the need for leaders willing to resort to ruthless power and violence to save the day. Similar currents were seen in literature and media in the lead-up to World War I, and then again in the 1950s as the spectre of communism and nuclear terror hovered threateningly over suburban tranquillity.[13] In these moments, there exists a feeling that if men get soft, the nation is placed in danger. Actor John Wayne's catalogue of films – Westerns and war adventures – captures this rugged masculinity required in a crisis. His conservative politics went hand in hand with a can-do approach to resisting perceived enemies and the role males are expected to play in the face of threat. Right-wing politics in more recent years reflects something of the same dynamic, as the 'strongman' has re-emerged as the desired leadership style for many voters in contested and polarised environments.

Time to listen

The confusion about how they are supposed to *be* can be crippling for boys and young men. Psychologist William Pollack, in his book *Real Boys' Voices*, interviewed American teenaged boys to try to investigate how they really feel. He was alarmed at what he found:

> I have discovered a glaring truth: America's boys are absolutely desperate to talk about their lives. They long to talk about things that are hurting them – their harassment from other boys, their troubled relationship with other boys, their embarrassment around girls and confusion about sex, their disconnection from parents, the violence that haunts them at school and on the street and their constant fear that they might not be as masculine as other boys.[14]

Pollack believes that all of this leads boys to construct a mask of masculinity. He describes this as a 'stance of male bravado and stoicism that many boys develop to cover their inner feelings of sadness, loneliness and vulnerability'.[15]

The Men's Project (an Australian initiative of Jesuit Social Services) conducted a 2018 and 2020 study into 1000 men aged 18–30. It found that men who live according to outdated and rigid

3. Models of Masculinity

masculine stereotypes – 'The Man Box' – are at significantly higher risk of using violence, online bullying and sexual harassment, as well as risky drinking and poor levels of mental health.[16] This project seeks to promote positive and healthy masculinities as a way to 'unpack' and dismantle that harmful 'man box'.

It is in everyone's interests for that to happen. Helping boys move towards a less prescribed idea of what it is to be male would be a start. And whether they choose 'the outdoor guy' or the 'tech expert', or some other identity or mix of identities, it doesn't matter. But a version of 'tender masculinity' – boys and men engaging with others, and with themselves, in positive, life-affirming patterns and behaviours – is a legitimate and achievable aim. (We will explore this notion in subsequent chapters.) There is work to do. Many boys are floundering and are coming up short in finding a workable answer to the question, 'What is it to be a man today?'

What is abundantly clear is that boys won't simply know how to be good men. They will have to be shown.

Re:CONSIDERING

4. MEN, MAYHEM AND MUTUAL BENEFIT

Taylor Swift's 2022 track 'Bejeweled', from her *Midnights* album, gives her take on the Cinderella story, but with a significant twist. The music video that accompanies the track portrays Swift as Cinderella escaping her evil stepsisters to attend a ball where, by winning a talent quest, someone will be given a castle, and a marriage proposal from the prince. Swift's character makes it to the ball, but this prince is someone she's dated before and been mistreated by. She wins the prize of course, but the traditional love story is jettisoned as she ditches the prince to take the castle for herself. Who needs a prince, right?

It's funny and ironic with a cleverly cynical contortion of a familiar tale. The prince in this case, played by Jack Antonoff, is deeply unappealing and gets what he deserves from his far superior 'subject'!

4. Men, Mayhem and Mutual Benefit

Taylor Swift is not averse to a revenge song, and she does them very well. But I wonder: could this piece of art reflect something of the changing cultural currents as well as the role and place of men today?

In April 2021, a female youth worker visiting Parkdale Secondary College in Melbourne's southeast conducted a seminar for Year 11 on diversity and inclusion. During the seminar she asked any white, male, Christian boy to stand up. She then proceeded to address these boys in front of the year group, telling them that they had to take responsibility for being 'oppressors' and 'privileged'. Understandably, this was met with outrage by parents. Hurried apologies were offered, and enquiries launched. It was an extreme case, but it left many (not least the boys themselves!) with a growing sense of unease. I know plenty of parents who hear stories like these and wonder about the future for their boys. What will be their place in the world?

Throughout much of history and across various cultures still, the preference for boys over girls is alarming. The sheer disappointment of parents in strongly patriarchal systems when the first gasps of a baby's breath come with the news 'It's a girl' is just one sign of the status women have had to endure. That may be changing in the West.

Fertility doctors in the United States claim that around 80% of prospective parents today who use gender selection techniques say they'd prefer a girl[1] as they can't ignore the brighter prospects for girls in a rapidly changing economic and social environment. There are four times the number of Google searches for 'foods to eat to conceive a girl' than 'foods to eat to conceive a boy'.[2] It's worth pondering the reasons for this, which are no doubt as complex as they are notable – and perhaps this is a moment to ask whether the answer to one terrible prejudice is to replace it with its opposite.

Toxic

The term 'toxic masculinity' is thrown around a lot these days.

We can all think of examples that fit the description, so we feel like we know what we and others mean by it. The term itself was hardly ever used prior to 2015, and even then, really only in a few academic journals. By 2017, after Donald Trump's political rise and the momentum of the #MeToo movement following revelations of the crimes of Harvey Weinstein and others, there were thousands of mentions in mostly mainstream media. But there is little agreement on a definition, and mostly the term is simply an indication of disapproval.[3] It now seems to refer to any male behaviour we don't like, whether it be truly monstrous or more trivial.[4]

Author and academic Richard Reeves, a Senior Fellow at the Brookings Institution in Washington, believes the term has the effect of poisoning the idea of masculinity itself. 'Toxic masculinity is a counterproductive term. Very few boys and men are likely to react well to the idea that there is something toxic inside them that needs to be exorcized,' he writes.[5] Reeves thinks this pejorative and lazily used language alienates the majority of men who are not violent or abusive while doing nothing to address the problem.

As painfully aware as I am of the dreadful behaviour of some men, when I hear 'toxic masculinity' being loosely thrown around, my thoughts sometimes drift to my weekend surfing mates. This is a group of (now) middle-aged men who have been meeting early on a Sunday morning for more than a decade to go for a surf together and then a coffee. About once a year, if someone can get organised enough to plan it, we go away for a weekend of surfing together. These guys are thoroughly decent blokes. They are committed to their families, to their community and to their work. They are excellent fathers and, as far as I can tell, imperfect but loving husbands. They are thoughtful, funny and kind. Some of them work at a soup kitchen at a church on a Monday night and have done for years. They are supportive of each other, emotionally intelligent and caring. Unlike the stereotype of the emotionally distant male unable to express his feelings, my friends are open about their struggles, accepting of advice and support and willing to make sacrifices for others who need help.

I also think of the male friends of my daughter and my son – both young adults. These boys come to our house often and we love having them around. They are as far from anything that could be described as 'toxic' as I could imagine. These are sensitive, kind, well-rounded boys, who love music and art and sport and go out of their way to encourage their friends and cheer them on in whatever it is they are into. They are young boys, so they no doubt sometimes say or do stupid things. They are learning. They seem remarkably open and inquisitive, accepting of difference and wanting to be decent human beings. Many of them have a great sense of humour. They are noticeably gentle souls.

There is potential for great good in all these people. If boys and men like these are receiving a message that their maleness is a problem, that is itself a problem.

Maybe we live in a bubble. No doubt all these qualities have emerged from a particular set of circumstances and in areas of some privilege and good fortune. They are the lucky ones with families and schools where they have been loved and nurtured and instructed and disciplined and shown what it looks like to live well.

But even that underlines my overall sense that most boys, placed in the right environment with strong role models and healthy cultures, will emerge as people we want to be around.

As we have seen, it's clear that not all young boys have those advantages.

Broken promises, lost dreams

Unfortunately, where we are at as a society with our boys and young men is mired in politics and culture wars in unhelpful ways. Richard Reeves believes the ideological commitments of both progressives and conservatives prevent them from addressing the issues boys are facing today. He says for conservatives, masculinity is the solution; for progressives, it's the problem. Progressives, he claims, want to deny any biological basis for sex differences, while conservatives want to give these differences more weight than they should. Conservatives might be more sympathetic to the challenges for males, but primarily as a way of returning to a past era of traditional care-giving females and male providers: 'The left tells men, "Be more like your sister". The right says, "Be more like your father." Neither is helpful.'[6] Reeves says it's noticeable that both the right and, more surprisingly, the left coalesce in their unwillingness to acknowledge structural problems that contribute to male dilemmas today. Instead, they place the blame squarely at the feet of individuals and their failures, whether in behaviour, health outcomes or educational attainment.[7]

But it's a complex story that finds men in the place they are in today. Susan Faludi's widely and deeply researched *Stiffed: The Betrayal of the American Man* offers many helpful diagnostic observations that apply much more broadly than just the United States.

Post-World War II men were, Faludi writes, offered a promise of steady work with solid homes, families and jobs, and a role to play in building the nation and mastering their domain. This promise, by century's end, had evaporated. The institutions they were meant to be loyal to for the rewards of

4. Men, Mayhem and Mutual Benefit

security and meaningful work had betrayed them.[8] Loss and disillusionment have been the result.

> A social pact between the nation's men and its institutions was collapsing, most prominently, but not exclusively, within the institutions of work. Masculine ideals of loyalty, productivity, and service lay in shards. Such codes were seen as passé and their male subscribers as vaguely pathetic. Loyalty meant you were too slow or too stupid to skip out on the company before it skipped out on you. Productivity was something corporations and their shareholders now measured not by employee elbow grease but by how many employees the company laid off. And service meant nothing more than consumer assistance, exemplified by a telemarketer trapped in a cubicle, a phone glued to his ear, his have-a-nice-day conversations preformulated and monitored.[9]

As jobs for men in industries like manufacturing have vanished, they have found their traditional role in the home hollowed out. While women have been able to challenge the many injustices that they have had to endure, over the same period men have found their spheres of influence and their stature diminishing.

As we noted in Chapter 2, in education the performance of girls has radically improved over the last 40 years. In 1975, the Australian Schools

Commission released a report that shone a light on the severe limits of opportunity for girls and sketched an alarming picture of sex-based inequality in Australia. This was a time when school was considered a training ground for girls to prepare for marriage and motherhood and not much else. At that point there was a lower percentage of girls than boys remaining at school to Year 12, subject choices for girls were extremely limited and males were much more represented in post-school education.

The report proved to be highly significant in changes that were to come, and in the years since, the situation has essentially been reversed. Census figures from 2020 reveal that 88% of girls stayed on to Year 12 compared with 79% for boys. In addition, 92% of women aged 20–24 had completed Year 12 or Certificate III or above compared with 87% of men.[10]

As girls continue to outshine their male counterparts in almost every subject in NSW's Higher School Certificate, in Victoria girls achieve an average Australian Tertiary Admissions Rank of 70.6 while the average for boys is 67.62. The pattern is repeated elsewhere and continues post-school too. A university admissions centre study found that boys were 'enrolling at lower rates, less likely to pass all their subjects and more likely to

4. Men, Mayhem and Mutual Benefit

fail everything'. The same study found that being male was 'greater than any of the other recognised disadvantages we looked at'.[11] Poorer writing skills appears to be a significant factor in these figures.

Attention is beginning to turn to the place of boys and what can be done to halt the decline. Differences in learning styles for boys and girls is frequently cited as significant, especially in terms of what happens in the classroom. A 2002 enquiry into the declining performance of boys noted the need for structure, discipline and clearly defined objectives and instructions for boys, with analytical and logical approaches to learning. But, as education expert Kevin Donnelly explains, Australian classrooms have for many years now adopted a more open-ended, enquiry-based approach that is less suited to boys.[12] The scarcity of male teachers – only 22% in schools (and less in primary school) – may be a factor as many boys look in vain for role models and mentors.

The careful, structured and deliberate moves to improve girls' education since the 1970s have produced remarkable results, and girls continue to shine and make the most of their opportunities. This is all good news. We now need to look to see what can be done for boys.

Andrew FitzSimons was the Principal of Dapto High School in the Illawarra region of New South

Wales for 20 years. He had a boys' mentor for the school and is on the board of the Top Blokes Foundation, which is dedicated to young men's wellbeing and mental health. He loves the way education now caters so well for girls but says that, as a principal, half a dozen initiatives and opportunities for girls would cross his desk each week, but almost nothing for boys. 'When I say we need to have programs to nurture boys, think about the different learning needs ... of boys, I'm told to sit in the corner.'[13]

Referring to education gaps, Francisco Ferreira, a professor of Inequality Studies at London School of Economics, recognises a problem that rightfully deserves attention: 'There is now wide consensus that gender inequalities are unfair, and lead to wasted human potential. That remains true when the disadvantaged are boys, as well as girls.'[14]

Control

Susan Faludi believes that the male predicament – whatever our political beliefs – stems from the notion that men, to be men, need to be in control. Women might consider the plight of men today and suspect that its source lies in the fact that their dominance and control has been challenged and they can't cope with that. A conservative might say women have gone too far and have taken control away from men. Both ideas rest on the assumption that being male is about holding the reins. 'The popular feminist joke that men are to blame for everything is just the flip side of the "family values" reactionary expectation that men should be in charge of everything,' writes Faludi. 'The problem is, neither of these views corresponds to how most men feel or to their actual positions in the world.'[15]

Faludi suggests that prior to 1800, men were judged primarily on their contribution to wider society, but as industrialisation took hold, a corresponding and useful (to burgeoning capitalism) mystique developed around the lone frontier figure as an emblem of virility and ambition. 'To be a man increasingly meant being ever on the rise, and the only way to know for sure you were rising was to claim control, and crush everyone and everything in your way.'[16]

Figures like Hollywood's Davy Crockett and even the advertising icon of the 70s and 80s, the Marlboro Man, are judged by the way they master and control their environments. Faludi fears that debates about male struggles today focus on how men are exercising or abusing their power but fail to consider whether men are, in fact, lacking a mooring and feeling out of control themselves:

> If men are the masters of their fate, what do they do about the unspoken sense that they are being mastered, in the marketplace and at home, by forces that seem to be sweeping away the soil beneath their feet? If men are mythologized as the ones who *make things happen*, then how can they begin to analyze what is happening to them?'[17]

Faludi senses that men, much like the women of the 1950s, are trapped in a box that's been created for them by the forces of the market and the relentless drive to make us all play consumer roles. Bolstered by the immensely powerful machinery of advertising, market forces invade all aspects of our lives such that even someone's masculinity is subject to commodification. The paradigm of modern masculinity is, writes Faludi, all about being the master of your universe, which neglects the extent to which men (like everyone) are subject to forces outside their control. Nor does it offer much as a way forward.

Nobody wins unless everybody wins

In the circumstances we've been describing, men can start to lose hope or look for someone to blame.

4. Men, Mayhem and Mutual Benefit

Who can they direct their grievances towards? A key element of this malaise is a lack of purpose, a declining sense of agency and a fear that they are no longer relevant. 'Without purpose, a boy often feels unneeded,' writes Warren Farrell. 'If he feels ashamed to admit that he feels unneeded – or doesn't know that's what he's feeling – he may also feel unheard and unseen.'[18] These feelings were common among working-class males who supported Donald Trump in the US and Brexit in the UK. When Trump became president, he achieved a 24-point lead among men – the widest in fifty years of exit polling. A particularly popular T-shirt at MAGA rallies read: 'I support Donald Trump. I love freedom. I drink beer. I turn wrenches. I protect my family. I eat meat and I own guns. If you don't like it MOVE.'[19] According to Richard Reeves, this drift to the political right among men is a pattern repeated around the world in places like Germany, Sweden and South Korea. Somewhere beneath all this unrest is a sense of confusion and a desire to reclaim something that's felt to have been lost.

There is undeniably a desire among men to address their needs. Whatever you make of Jordan Peterson, the Canadian psychologist who shot to media and publishing fame from 2016 with his *12 Rules for Life*, he clearly hit a nerve. The book sold 5 million copies, and Peterson believes around 80% of his audience are young men, who now pack out large auditoriums and theatres to hear him speak. In the foreword to the book, Dr Norman Doidge suggests its popularity is at least partly related to an age of moral relativism that has created a kind of nihilism that doesn't satisfy. We might wish to be free of rules, but ultimately we need structure and guidelines to allow us all to flourish. Here is an appeal to think carefully about questions of virtue – the search for wisdom, justice and the good life. Peterson speaks into that void and the response is truly remarkable.

There are more unsavoury responses to the male predicament that also garner large audiences. Andrew Tate is a former kickboxer and reality TV personality. Before his banning from several social media platforms and then arrest in December 2022 on charges of human trafficking, organised crime and rape (allegations he denies), Tate had become an internet star with an enormous following, spouting misogynistic comments and what many would consider hate speech. Tate offered his legion of young male fans a recipe for making money, attracting women and establishing a (menacing) presence. The whole schtick was one of control, racism, simmering violence and a threatening dominance of women. In videos that were watched millions of times, he said things like 'I inflict, I expect, absolute loyalty from my woman … I ain't having my chicks talking to other dudes, liking other dudes. My chicks don't go to the club without me, they are at home.'[20]

That feels so barbaric it's hard to believe anyone takes it seriously. But evidently many do. Videos tagged #AndrewTate have been watched 12 billion times.[21] A friend tells me that a school he recently spoke at is dismayed at how many of their teenaged boys are captivated by Tate. The women at the school understandably feel threatened. The potential for radicalisation of disaffected young men is frighteningly clear.

According to the writer Caitlin Flanagan, many boys find Tate appealing because they have absorbed a message that masculinity is 'a dangerous and suspicious and possibly socially constructed fantasy that they must cast off in every way', and they react against that.

'If we don't give these boys positive examples of strength as a virtue, they will look elsewhere,' Flanagan writes.[22] Simply suppressing the energy, boldness and orientation towards action that is broadly characteristic of boys doesn't work. Understanding and channelling these naturally occurring traits in positive directions can.

The answer to all that is challenging for boys

and men today is not a return to the past of male domination and limitations on female empowerment. Who would want that? As long ago as 1958, Arthur Schlesinger Jr, in an essay for *Esquire* titled 'The Crisis of American Masculinity', wrote:

> The key to recovery of masculinity does not lie in any wistful hope of humiliating the aggressive female and restoring the old masculine supremacy. Masculine supremacy, like white supremacy, was the neurosis of an immature society. It is good for men as well as for women that women have been set free.[23]

That much, we hope, is clear. Things have improved immeasurably for women, especially in the West. Huge strides have been taken in affording opportunities for girls to thrive, even if there is a long way to go on that journey. What is increasingly clear is that we need boys and men to flourish alongside women and girls. As Susan Faludi reflects, 'If my travels taught me anything about the two sexes, it is that each of our struggles depends on the success of the other's.'[24]

Re:CONSIDERING

5. SIGNS OF LIFE

When I was a very young teacher, for my first job, I arrived at a boys' school in the city from a country university to teach history. Part of my duties involved coaching rugby and cricket, which I loved doing. I remember immediately being amazed by a boy in Year 12 who was fullback in the First XV rugby team, a member of the First XI cricket team and who also happened to be a virtuoso violinist and a top student. He was an exceptional kid of course, and there weren't too many as accomplished as him, but I remember thinking he would simply be inconceivable at my old school. The horizons of what could be imagined there were so meagre by comparison.

I had found myself in a place where there was a deliberate attempt to celebrate and foster a wide set of skills, abilities and interests, and it was entirely natural for boys to seek to develop those interests no matter what they were. It was a robust male environment, but being male didn't just mean one thing.

Early in my time there I was also fortunate enough to be present on the day when two decidedly unsporty and 'uncool' Year 12 boys stood before a packed assembly hall and sang the most exquisitely beautiful operatic duet – and received a prolonged and heartfelt standing ovation from the whole school. An old science and drama teacher sitting next to me had tears streaming down his face by the end of the item. Everyone present recognised the immense skill and talent before us. You couldn't miss the dedication required to be able to deliver a performance of such soaring beauty, and everybody knew it was only right to cheer, and cheer loudly!

I don't want to overclaim here. This was an imperfect environment and no doubt it contained some of the regrettable elements of masculinity that we have already discussed, but my time at that school – about ten years in the end – gave me a powerful illustration of what is possible with concerted, intentional, organised efforts to nourish the best in young men.

Evolution

I was at the school as an educator, but I was also being educated about wider and deeper possibilities for being a male. So much has changed in recent decades in that regard. The huge, positive shifts in the status and role of women have brought about necessary adjustments in the way men exist in the world.

One conspicuous way is how involved in children's lives many men are these days. With most couples both working in some capacity, and with parenting duties also being shared, young fathers are heavily engaged in the raising of their children. That wasn't the case when I was a boy. I had (and have) a great dad who was always loving and engaged with us. But he was from a different era. He wasn't present for the births of any of his three boys (men weren't allowed anywhere near the action in those days). The first nappy he changed was my daughter's, his grandchild's. Cooking and cleaning were very much my mum's domain, even though she worked as well. I don't remember either of them playing with us kids in anything like the way I have spent time with my own children.

Steve Biddulph, a psychologist who has written about boys and men for decades, recognises that real changes have taken place and that men are much more involved in their kid's lives today. But he thinks those same men don't always know what to pass on because they had no experience of it.

Someone who is addressing that gap is Andrew McUtchen. He is the co-creator of The Father Hood, an online community that supports dads to take on the challenge of being the best dad they can be. Father to three girls aged 8, 9 and 10, along with an older stepdaughter, Andrew believes this is the best time in history to be a dad. Being more emotionally and actively involved in the family is hugely rewarding, but he is conscious that his own dad wasn't able to give him much guidance in this regard.

> I'd say, 'Dad, how did you deal with it when your wife was [busy] and you had two nappies to change at once?' And he's like, 'I've got nothing to tell you … I can't help you out. It's another world.'

But McUtchen's dad was committed to the family and emotionally present, and that set Andrew up for the era he finds himself in, where being a father has given him a reason to be a better person:

> I don't think I've ever been as motivated to be as positive a male as I am as a dad, because I have three daughters looking up to me every day, and

5. Signs of Life

> I'm trying to live my best life and I'm trying to show them the kind of man that men can be. So, I have inspiration every day to do that.[1]

McUtchen would find support on that front from author Richard Reeves, who believes that we all need to recognise that the old model of fatherhood – narrowly based on economic provision, with the assumption of an unencumbered spouse – is unfit for a world of gender equality. It needs replacing with more expansive roles for fathers – including a much bigger caring element that is on equal footing with mothers, sharing not only provision for the family but also the caring aspects. This involves broadening the definition of what it means to be a father.[2] Equal and independent parental leave, a modernised child support system and father-friendly employment opportunities are needed for this to become a reality. It's a task worth taking on.

Steve Biddulph firmly believes that men today face the challenge of escaping the prison of loneliness, compulsive competition and lifelong emotional timidity. The loneliness comes from endlessly feeling the need to put on a mask – perhaps of control and steadfastness or some other role – for the benefit of those around them, without ever therefore feeling known and loved. The competition is linked to loneliness and stems from treating others with mistrust. Emotional timidity is the result of limited emotional language and the burying of feelings due to various subtle and direct forms of socialisation. It's an unhealthy mix, Biddulph believes.

Men making a change

Since his book *Manhood* was first published in 1994, Steve Biddulph has witnessed significant steps forward. In the 90s he wrote about the straitjacket of Australian mateship that took the form of an unspoken code that limited what men could say to each other, didn't make room for difference and was unable to express love.

Revisiting the topic 25 years later in his book *The New Manhood* (2019), Biddulph shows how much has changed. Now men hug at airports, express grief and joy, have deeper friendships and can even say they love each other. These are welcome developments. Biddulph has witnessed the rapid growth of men's groups and reports of serious emotional healing in these contexts. When men are able to experience the love and affection of other men, it is possible for them to get past the need for competitiveness and be more

5. Signs of Life

open to serving others and nurturing good things, writes Biddulph.[3]

Particularly the more informal men's groups seem to have lasting benefit. Unlike some of the clubs that are about building a reputation in business or making connections, initiatives like the Men's Shed movement – with over 900 groups in Australia, Ireland, Finland and Greece – allow for vulnerability and unvarnished connection through shared activity and conversation.

Former Sydney Swans AFL star Tadhg Kennelly acknowledges being dragged out of a mental slump by his friend David Eccles at a time when he really needed it. Eccles, who saw this as mutual support, says, 'We kind of realised that our wives would go to coffee with a friend and they would know everything about each other. But men, we go to the pub and we chat about the football but we don't really know anything about each other.' Together they formed When No One's Watching (WNOW), a group that meets at the beach for a workout, a dip and most importantly, a coffee afterwards to connect with each other. It grew from a few friends to now more than 200 men at Maroubra and other locations as well. The pair have plans to eventually involve one million men in the community. They were awarded the NSW Mental Health Commission's community champion award for their service to men's mental health. The mental health commissioner Catherine Lourey said the group was 'an excellent example of how peer support can make a real difference in people's lives when they are facing the challenges of loneliness, isolation, and anxiety, all of which are contributing factors to increased vulnerability to suicide.' She praised the men for facilitating spaces where men could express emotions and talk about problems, building personal networks and resilience.[4]

The challenge and reward of honesty and openness

Matt Andrews is in his mid-fifties and is an expert in strategic communications. A few years ago, he had something of a breakdown following a divorce from his long-time partner that Matt says was entirely his fault. The breakup of his relationship was a terrible shock, and it made him face his demons that were complex and deep-seated. Among other things, he found significant support in a men's group therapy initiative that he describes as transformative. Andrews says in learning to relate well with other men, he was finally able to make some progress in his personal development:

> It really wasn't until I was part of that men's group, which was meeting once a week for a couple of hours, that I really started to see changes in me and that other people, including my former wife and children, have said that no, you've actually started to change, particularly when it comes to matters of anger and aggression.[5]

Andrews says there are vital ingredients in these men's support groups that if missing make them a waste of time in making real change. The number one ingredient is honesty – 'honesty of the heart' as he puts it. Not just knowing someone's opinions or even things that have happened to them, but true openness.

> Imagine if you tell me, 'I once punched a boy in the face in Year 7,' well now I know something about you. But what if then you say, 'I once punched a boy in the face in Year 7 and it made me really happy, and now I feel guilty about it,' it's like, OK, now we've got an encounter.

It's that level of engagement that's required. Another key ingredient for these groups to work, then, is confidentiality and a commitment to the good of other people – along with permission to share really dark emotions with another man, in order to make sense of those emotions and to move ahead.

Andrews confesses that he was among those in his group who have said and done terrible things that have been costly to his family. The biggest change, he argues, comes from taking responsibility for it. 'When a man is able to say, "I did that. It's on me. It's not my wife's fault. It's not the fault of one of my business partners, one of my children, it's me" … that's when progress and growth can take place.'

Changing our definitions

The men's group phenomenon is an encouraging sign. Yet it also tends to focus on dealing with the damage and fallout from inadequate formative experiences for boys and men, and the need for healing. Attending to earlier stages in a young man's development with a broader, clearer, more positive definition of manhood is a crucial piece of this puzzle too.

Joe Ehrmann was a successful NFL defensive lineman for the Baltimore Colts in the 1970s, and these days, as well as being a pastor, he spends his time writing and speaking about healthy

5. Signs of Life

masculinity. His father, a former boxer, provided him with a very old-school definition of manhood that amounted to learning to dominate other people and circumstances without consideration of your feelings or those of others. That was some help on the football field, but it didn't prepare him well at all for crises like the death of his teenaged brother from cancer when Ehrmann was 29.

In an interview with National Public Radio, he explained that this loss was the beginning of a quest for answers to deep questions of meaning and purpose:

> I was 29 years old, I was six years into my NFL career, and I had no concept – no concept what life was about, and no concept what I was about. And on this journey, I ended up asking the question: What does it mean to be a man? ...
>
> I recognized that everything I had invested my life in – all my accomplishments, my achievements, the stuff I had accumulated – I recognized at that moment they offered no hope or help to my ... 18-year-old brother lying on his deathbed. ...
>
> All I had was these old 'man up' kind of things – 'suck it up, we'll get through this together' – when he [Ehrmann's brother] really needed the emotional, the nurturing, the love. And I had to really struggle to pull that out of my heart.[6]

Ehrmann believes the great lie of masculinity boils down to three things. Firstly, it's tied to athletic ability – size and strength. Secondly, it's associated with sexual conquests – using other people for your own benefit. And thirdly, economic success – the size of your wallet and the power associated with that. This definition is not only incredibly limited and limiting, but most men don't feel like they measure up. It is this subsequently painful sense of inadequacy that Ehrmann believes men will typically soothe with alcohol, drugs, materialism or porn.

Replacing that definition with something more helpful is a decades-long process. For Ehrmann, it must centre around two things:

- *Relationships*: the ability to love and be loved. Asking ourselves questions like 'What kind of husband am I (or could I be)? What kind of son? Friend? Colleague?' The focus needs to be on nurturing healthy relationships and cultivating things like compassion, empathy, respect, and kindness.
- *Commitment to a cause*: finding ways to make the world a better place, always with attention to people and relationships and improving the lives of others.[7]

5. Signs of Life

These two areas are where Joe Ehrmann believes our energies should be focused, and they essentially boil down to being a man for others. Being a person who, rather than exhibiting the lone-wolf characteristics of traditional maleness, attends to his life in such a way that it makes other people's lives better.

Books such as *Real Boys*, by psychologist William Pollack, and *Raising Cain: Protecting the Emotional Life of Boys*, by Dan Kindlon and Michael Thompson, each make the case for helping boys develop a full emotional repertoire. These authors believe it is entirely possible to create environments where boys can be physically active and vigorous without having to suppress their expressive, loving, tender natures. Pollack says boys need to be able to express the full range of emotions – fear, sadness, disappointment – and to know that these are normal and fit with being a man.[8] Male modelling of a rich emotional life with a male identity is a crucial part of this process. Boys need to experience empathy at home and school in order to establish emotional connections and build close supportive relationships.[9]

Positive visions

Daniel Principe is a young man on a mission. Up until recently he worked with an organisation called Collective Shout that has campaigned for over ten years against the sexualisation and exploitation of girls and women. Collective Shout describes its work as resisting the 'pornification of culture and the way its messages have become entrenched in mainstream society, presenting distorted and dishonest ideas about women and girls, sexuality and relationships.'[10]

Principe's ongoing work is to travel around to schools and other communities to talk, especially to the boys, about respect for girls and women, the pitfalls of pornography and ways to reimagine healthy expressions of masculinity. He explains to me that he is painfully aware of the pressure on young men still to fit into a narrow definition of being male. He notices a 'performative callousness' of boys in front of their peers, that often betrays the way individual boys truly feel. He'll often ask a gathering of school students if they've ever experienced a situation where a boy is being really nice to them, but when another boy enters the room, things change and they suddenly become mean. 'Every hand goes up. Male and female,' says Principe. This is performing for watching eyes and is mostly about insecurities and fears, he believes.

Principe likes to challenge boys to think about how their behaviour impacts those around them, urging them towards more respect for girls – acknowledging their full humanity, kindness to others and 'a more fulsome way to embody what it is to be a man'. He says that most boys respond very positively to such a challenge. He has heard from groups of boys, after experiencing his presentation, who have taken it upon themselves to go and apologise to girls they have not treated well in the past.[11]

An unforgettable moment for Principe, that he recounted in an interview with *The Sydney Morning Herald*, occurred during one of his sessions at a rural school in New South Wales and is illustrative of what he believes is possible. A previously very quiet 11-year-old boy spoke up to tell the group that at his last school his peers had daily encouraged him to take his own life:

> He sat there in front of his mates. He started to get choked up, his eyes welled up. One of the other boys in the front row got up and sat next to him, and just put his hand on his back. And then another boy from the other side of the room got up and sat on the other side. And those two

boys just sat there for the rest of that session, comforting him, there with him, in that emotion and that experience. ...

'It was the most profound moment, I would almost argue, in my life ... That was everything to witness. In those moments are some of the most beautiful things I've ever seen happen. I wish the rest of the world could witness it.'[12]

Principe is under no illusions as to how big a challenge it is to steer young men in a good direction, but he is upbeat and positive about what can be done by appealing to boys' better natures and inviting them into a better vision of themselves.

Re:CONSIDERING

6. REMEDIES

The immensely popular television series *Ted Lasso* ended after three seasons of viewers being exposed to the homely wisdom and perpetual positivity of American Ted Lasso coaching an English Premier League football club despite knowing virtually nothing about the game itself. The unlikely set-up enabled a story of heart-warming contrast to real-life professional sport where conquest, domination and ruthless competitiveness is replaced with concern for personal growth, emotional maturity, selflessness, friendship and true community. And above all, kindness.

It was pretty cheesy, and sometimes unnecessarily crude, but it had some golden moments. A central character, Roy Kent, a recently retired player-turned-coach is perpetually and comically angry, inarticulate, representing the emotionally stunted and bewildered male unable to understand or cope with his own or anyone else's emotions. But even Roy can't escape the relentless kindness of Lasso, and by the end he is honestly wrestling with his own inadequacies and looking for solutions and wanting to be 'someone better'. 'Can people change?' he asks. Aided by the support of male friends, and an insightful psychologist, he is on a journey towards wholeness. The lesson of the show seems to be that, until Lasso came along, this group of young men didn't really have anyone invested in showing them how to be good men. But when they did, many things worth celebrating flowed into their lives.

So, having surveyed some of the challenges boys and men are facing and considered some green shoots of change occurring, we turn now to ways to water those green shoots and create environments in which boys and young men are likely to mature in productive directions.

The river of knowledge

Steve Biddulph believes that where there is chaos in men's lives, it is often due to a lack of three things: affection (letting boys know they matter), teaching (helping them to understand their lives) and example (earning by observation how a good man feels, thinks and acts).

6. Remedies

He notes that it's still the case that most of the rearing of boys is done by women – their mothers and then female teachers. There's nothing wrong with that, he says, but he believes boys need males who know how to drive the male body and mind. They benefit from hundreds of hours of time spent with men who can show restraint, patience, control, empathy, kindness, generosity and humour, and show how those things are desirable and admirable.[1]

When I read that list, I can't help being reminded of what was missing in the school environment I experienced as a boy. The metaphor Biddulph uses is one of a river of knowledge that you receive and grow strong in, then pass on downstream to others. You are connected through an inherited masculinity born of wisdom, time and experience. Biddulph thinks other cultures are better at this than we are in the West, and we need to pay attention to the lessons to be learned elsewhere.

Anthropologist David Gilmore's cross-cultural study of manliness, *Manhood in the Making: Cultural Concepts of Masculinity*, showed that almost all societies had a concept of 'real', 'true' and 'adult' manhood that was seen as essential to its society's wellbeing. One essential element was the need for boys to be ushered into manhood by other men.[2]

Of course, it matters what is being passed on. There are plenty of 'rivers' depositing poisonous examples of what we mean by becoming a man. Joe Ehrmann thinks team sports are an excellent place to help boys become good men, but only when the coach sees his or her role as positively influencing the arc of a young person's life by modelling, nurturing and teaching character. 'You teach them how to build authentic community as men caring for and loving each other,' says Ehrmann.[3] He is well aware of sports cultures where the opposite is the case and where the players are used for the selfish ends of the coach's ambitions.

Community and building the village

When I was a teenager, my entire life revolved around sport – playing it, practising it, watching it. In a way it was all I really cared about. Meanwhile my dad and mum could not have been less interested. They just weren't into sport at all, and it was not something they had any understanding of. They would drop me off at my games and drive off without ever thinking of staying to watch. It just didn't occur to them. Supportive from a distance, you might say.

6. Remedies

But two of my dad's good friends were as sports-mad as I was. They knew I was into it, and whenever they came to our house or saw me at a function or a family get-together, they would always take the time to ask me about my games. They'd want to know my latest efforts – my successes and failures. They'd press me for details and show a genuine interest in what I was doing. One of them would take me and my brothers out for games of golf. The other, who played cricket and baseball at a high level, would grab my cricket bat and offer some very technical advice. I also was fortunate enough to have a few older boys I admired who paid attention to me and were kind and encouraging.

And here's the thing. That was enough. Having an adult or two who are not your parents show interest in you gives you the impression that you are someone who is worth having around. It builds you up and makes you feel special. It's something I have tried to carry into my own adult life, to offer something similar to my kids' friends and my friends' kids. It doesn't take much effort, but it can make a huge difference in a young person's life. It did in mine.

We need communities to raise healthy boys and not place the sole responsibility on parents.

In 2018, an enormous study was released in the United States on race and economic opportunity. Conducted by researchers at Harvard, Stanford and the Census Bureau, it tracked the economic fortunes and misfortunes of millions of children born in America between 1978 and 1983. It revealed alarming impacts of racism on outcomes for black boys particularly. But what was fascinating about that study was that it clearly revealed the positive impact of the presence of fathers in a given neighbourhood. This was true even for boys whose own fathers were not around. Just having a good number of fathers around them was enough to make a statistically significant difference in terms of how well the boys fared.[4]

Professor Bruce Robinson has many strings to his bow, including being an expert in the detection of asbestos-induced lung cancer, mesothelioma. But he's also been a successful Australian rules football player and coach, and was the founder of the Fathering Project, a movement to support fathers and father figures to be the best parent they can be so that their children can thrive. Robinson has great interest in how boys can do well and what things hinder their development. We need good fathers, but also good father figures, he tells me.[5] 'Boys have always learned in an apprenticeship to their father or another father figure, whether they are out hunting or ploughing the fields,' he says. Values need to be taught and more importantly modelled, says Robinson. Ideally, they will come from a variety of sources and not only your parents.

The key values, he says, that pretty much everyone can agree on, are firstly, respect: you have to respect everybody. Respect for girls and women is a crucial lesson to learn. Secondly, integrity: 'Teach your sons that you will not tolerate a lack of integrity … I used to say to my kids, you know, someone could take over this country and put us all in concentration camps. They can take away your freedom, your food, your clothes, but they can't take away your integrity. Only you can give that away. Never give it away.' Thirdly, Robinson says teaching boys the value of kindness as a crucial virtue will serve us all well.

It is within a web of relationships that these things are taught most effectively.

Andrew FitzSimons, long-time Principal at Dapto High, is a big believer in mentorship programs for boys and believes some of the most impressive progress made at his school has come from intentional initiatives in this area. 'My rule of thumb is the mentor knows your birthday and you know his or hers. So, you have someone that's not your principal, not your boss, not your Mum or your Dad, somebody who is slightly to one side, who is your advocate and cares about you,' says FitzSimons.[6]

Structure and personal responsibility

The modern West's highest value today appears to be 'freedom' – and there is much that is laudable in that. But a problem might be that our definition of that freedom has evolved to a point where it represents little more than endless choice, and anything that might hinder that endless choice is anathema. It's a hollowed-out definition that previous generations would find novel. By contrast, they were soaked in an understanding of freedom and flourishing that involved making good choices, recognising that some paths are more beneficial than others and that wisdom was needed to discern those paths. Sometimes choosing the harder thing was the better choice on the road to a free and happy life. Importantly, these choices involved not just reaching within yourself to conjure up whatever strength of insight you might have, but being guided by a community

6. Remedies

and consulting those more experienced than you as you engaged in tried-and-true practices that had been passed down. It involved a lot more than self-reflection or self-discovery.

It's no doubt unpopular to say it these days, but the kind of thinking that promotes expressive individualism over all else hasn't served us well. And boys especially, in their formative years, need structure, guidance and firm boundaries. They don't need oppressive, strict and cruel discipline that squashes their uniqueness and produces compliant clones. We've moved past that. But they still need limits that are protective, firmly established and somewhat demanding, and with consequences when lines are transgressed. And as much as they protest these limits, experienced educators will tell you, deep down, most boys are glad when those limits are there. It makes them feel safe. It makes them feel the grown-ups are in charge. It's an important thing to know while you are still maturing.

This is true in both school and family life, where an abandonment of firm structure and expectation always proves a fraudulent friend for growing boys. In Chapter 4 I mentioned the spectacular and, frankly, hugely surprising popularity, especially with young men, of Jordan Peterson's *12 Rules for Life*. Peterson's blunt and demanding call to personal responsibility and refusal to adopt a victim mentality has resonated with many. That is something to pay attention to.

I have taught in a number of different environments and witnessed very different approaches to boundaries and discipline. I've seen what happens when it's all too harsh and restrictive, where an atmosphere of fear is the dominant controlling mechanism. Resentment and anger naturally flow out of such places.

I've also witnessed school communities where standards were very loose, where staff were concerned to never to upset the children and where all power appeared to reside with the teenagers. In those cases, it seemed obvious to me that the kids were taking the adults for a ride. It was chaotic and unpleasant for anyone but the loudest, most obnoxious students present.

A middle ground of strong boundaries that are enforced, combined with enthusiastic encouragement, nurture and interest in each student as an individual, serves everyone well. And it's achievable. I have seen it. This is true of course for girls as well as boys. It might be even more important for boys, though. Like any good game, where everyone involved knows the rules and how to play within them, there is huge scope for fun, self-expression and mutual benefit within well-marked lines.

Calculated risk

I am naturally a cautious person, but when I was backpacking around the world for a year in the mid-90s, I did seem to develop a more carefree, give-it-a-crack attitude than I would normally be known for. By the time I got to Zimbabwe towards the end of that year, I found myself enthusiastically embracing the 111-metre bungy jump at Victoria Falls, white-water rafting the Grade 5 rapids on the crocodile-infested Zambezi River and swimming in a rock pool right on the edge of Vic Falls, with friends holding my legs so I could peer over the abyss. It was all fabulous fun. Looking back, I now consider some of this to have been a bit reckless. I suspect the most danger I was in might have been on the local buses, travelling long distances between towns. These trips were a bit hair-raising. Or hitchhiking into Hwange National Park when, casually waiting beside a tree on a vast plain in hope of a ride, an African woman told me and my friends that she was afraid of the lions in the area where we were standing! Naivety can sometimes be your friend.

The point is, life is full of risk. We are fragile creatures, and things can and do sometimes go wrong. But to really embrace life, you have to be able to take on some calculated risks. The equation for that calculation will be different for different people, and it clearly can become an exercise in carelessness that endangers your own life and the lives of others. But it is vital to our growth as people that we step out into the world in a manner that opens the possibility of encounter with the richness of experience that life can offer.

Stereotypical male behaviour is known to involve risk-taking, and that is often a criticism. Teaching boys and young men to take calculated risk – risk that involves an assessment of potential benefits but also the costs to themselves and others, and sometimes having the sense to say no – is an essential exercise in their development. But so too is taking some risks and surviving them – channelling energy and vitality into activities that balance risk and reward, and finding that some of these challenges are exciting and life-giving. Boys need shepherding in ways that don't quash their natural affinity for risk. Even if we need to pray hard as we release them into the world.

6. Remedies

Rites of passage

A process that ushers a boy from childhood into adulthood is a common human experience across the ages. It might involve surviving a period of time in the wilderness or carrying out your first successful hunting mission. But it can also mean getting blind drunk, losing control and vomiting in the gutter. Entry into the adult world can be tawdry or noble depending on the context.

Long-time headmaster of a boys' school Dr Timothy Wright thinks a physical challenge of some sort can be a useful exercise in this regard. That might involve outdoor education or sport, but a cultural challenge – like preparing and delivering a speech, or learning to sing or perform a drama or play an instrument for an audience – can also form part of the process. Even a group of fathers taking their boys away on a camping trip or some other kind of getaway and talking to them about being young men – the challenges and joys and ways to navigate this stage of life well. Wright believes the need to face a challenge is absolutely essential in the process. 'If you've never faced a challenge and overcome it, I don't think that you're an adult,' he says.[7]

Franciscan monk Richard Rohr, a popular writer on spirituality, believes rites of passage form a vital spiritual practice, passing on wisdom to the young and helping them be contributors to their community. He identifies five key things to understand about life in the process of becoming a good man. Firstly, facing the fact that you are going to die one day – something Rohr believes we are very good at avoiding – helps give you healthy perspective on the way you are living *now*. Related to that sobering lesson is recognising and embracing the fact that life is going to be hard. If full and rich living is your goal, expect some pain. Thirdly, learning that, in the big scheme of things, you are not that important – a view that runs counter to most of the cultural currents we find ourselves in. Fourthly, coming to understand that life is not all about you, and being comfortable with not being the centre of all things, frees you up to a life of service to others. This is a key aspect of initiation rites. Lastly, coming to understand that you are not ultimately in control of the outcome is part of the road to maturity.[8]

In life, we are to seek the good and work hard towards it, but for men who like control and to be able to 'fix' things, it's important to recognise that often what we hope for is beyond our reach and that it's the doing rather than the result that matters. Each of these lessons form a healthy initiation into manhood.

Positive peer pressure

We all know the perils of peer pressure that can lead even the most seemingly sensible boys to careen off in calamitous directions. There wouldn't be many men who couldn't put down to peer pressure occasions where they have said or done things they regret.

But it doesn't have to be that way. Not only can we train boys to resist the worst elements of peer group bluster and boofheadedness, but we can create circumstances where the influence of peers can steer groups in favourable directions. Youth advocate Daniel Principe is a firm believer in the potential for peer group dynamics to harness boys' spiritedness. Pack mentality can undoubtedly be a negative. But does it have to be?

> I'm always asking, 'Could that be a disruptive force for good? Could that be something that disrupts bullying? Could that be something that seeks out and reaches out to a kid that's being excluded? Could that be the force that barges into a room at a party where a girl's being taken

advantage of ... could we actually channel that masculine energy?'[9]

For that kind of potential action to become reality, a strong foundation of taught and ingrained virtues needs to have been imparted to enough of the group for it to make a difference. Modelling, mentorship and careful direction given by parents, other adults, coaches, communities and educational settings all play a vital part. I don't think it's overly starry-eyed to hope for this kind of outcome.

HEAL jobs

As discussed in Chapter 4, the labour market has changed so much in recent decades and so many manufacturing and heavy-industry jobs have evaporated that many men have been left behind and lost what they once relied upon for stability. What might be a solution? Richard Reeves suggests that huge opportunities lie in the sector known as HEAL – health, education, administration and literacy – and that this could be a pathway for many men to consider, especially as traditional understandings of the male role broaden and evolve. We need men in this sector, such as in teaching and nursing. There are jobs to be found, and these jobs tend to be less vulnerable to economic downturn. Moves to make the sector more attractive with pipelines in the education system, programs to reduce the stigma of men's involvement in these fields and financial incentives to get men engaged would all be beneficial.[10]

Restitution and recovery

Timothy Wright is a strong believer in discipline and boys learning about the consequences of their actions. But he doesn't think that's the whole picture. There needs to be another layer to engage with boys meaningfully and productively:

> I think we need to say we all have faults, and I think one of the things we need to be always saying is when young people make mistakes, is that we need to be clear that that's not acceptable … [But] I think we don't do well in society, particularly in society fed by media hounds that really want to rip people apart, if we don't deal with the fact that everybody makes mistakes, and there needs to be a way back. At the gym I'm going to there are a couple of young guys who've done

> time in jail. And as I listen to them talk, they're at the gym because there's actually nobody who will give them a job. And I don't think these guys have probably done much more than sell a bit of dope or stolen a car. Now I'm not saying those things are trivial but at the same time, I wouldn't like to be held responsible for every idiotic thing I did at 18 or 19. And so culturally, I think one of the things we do is we're very quick to condemn men when they've made a mistake and say, 'That's it, you know? You're dead to us' one way or the other. And it's just not realistic.[11]

In other words, boys and young men need grace, forgiveness and a way back when they have transgressed. Again, community is vital in that negotiated space of accountability, acceptance and restoration.

There's no doubt many boys and young men these days wake up and look out at the world with some confusion. Who and what are they supposed to be? What will deliver them the life they long for, and what even is the shape of that life? But there are also positive signs and good stories about where young males have come to, often outstripping their dads in emotional intelligence and emotional literacy, and showing a dexterity in navigating the complex world they find themselves in. And there are ingredients, many that are not new, that are available and clearly enhance the likelihood of a young boy developing in a good direction.

For this to happen physical, emotional, psychological and spiritual needs all require attention. To complete our discussion, we now turn to contemplate some ancient spiritual wisdom as another vital piece in this complicated puzzle.

Re:CONSIDERING

7. ANCIENT WISDOM FOR MODERN TIMES

There's an urgent need for a positive vision of masculinity today that is realistic, appealing and achievable – one that can capture the minds, hearts and emotions of boys and men of all ages in a manner that benefits everyone.

I hope I have been able to convey a sense of the many different flavours and shapes that masculinity comes in and should come in. But it's also clear that any suggestions for change and growth have to be things that men can relate to. A picture of being male that opens up horizons of possibilities that are life-giving and energising, while being socially beneficial, is a goal worth striving for.

Love as a framework

When I was young, I don't think I ever heard men talk about love (unless they meant romantic love).

7. Ancient Wisdom for Modern Times

I didn't hear men tell their children that they loved them (even when they did). I didn't ever hear men tell their mates that they loved them. They showed love indirectly, in that bantering Australian way. But they always stopped short of articulating their love. All that had an impact on me, and I must have absorbed the message that for some reason men don't talk like that. It left an awkwardness that I probably didn't get past until I had my own kids.

I once interviewed Australian Test cricketer and coach Justin Langer, who talked about how hard it was as an Australian bloke to tell your dad that you loved him. That was a topic of conversation one night with his teammates while away on tour and, after a few beers, he called his dad to tell him he loved him. His dad initially didn't know what to say! But once they'd broken that ice, it became more natural after that.

Educator Timothy Wright thinks we need the 'lens of love' to talk about the way to behave, and that even now that is too rare. Usually discourse about how we organise society involves rights and responsibilities but rarely the obligation to love. This, he argues, is what men and boys need.[1]

The issue of consent is perhaps a good example of this. In recent years it has become clear that education around consent and the rules of engagement when it comes to sex are vital for respect and healthy interaction. That lesson has emerged from too many terrible stories of mistreatment and abuse. Boys and young men evidently need this spelled out loudly and clearly to them, and it's good that is happening now.

But it's fair to ask: is 'consent' enough? Plenty of commentators are suggesting we need deeper and richer categories to help navigate such troubled waters. Writing for *The Washington Post* about consent, Christine Emba appeals to 'love' – and particularly 13th-century philosopher and theologian Thomas Aquinas' conception of love as 'willing the good of the other', or building goodwill toward another for the sake of that person and not oneself.[2] This is about caring for other people to the extent that you focus on how your action (or inaction) might affect them. The approach that Emba advocates stands in stark contrast to relationships that are self-centred and all about what I can get out of them. The benefits of a more selfless attitude when it comes to sexual relationships – and of course not only sexual relationships – are many.

As I've engaged with this topic and read and spoken to experts – psychologists, educationalists, philosophers and coaches – on the subject of healthy masculinity, they all end up talking about virtues that, taken together, add up to the notion of being 'a man for others'. The vision is one of deploying whatever power or skill or ability you might have – whether physical, artistic, intellectual, social or emotional – in the service of other people. It's a re-imagining of power and gaining a sense of the full life to be found, not in the service of our own wants, but in elevating those around us. It's about love in the fullest sense of the word. Any kind of boy or man can aspire to love of that nature.

But truthfully, it's a counterintuitive and countercultural message. It needs a foundation to support it and a story to sustain it.

Authority and vulnerability

American author Andy Crouch's book *Strong and Weak: Embracing a Life of Love, Risk, and True Flourishing*, presents an argument that's relevant to our aspirations for boys and men. Crouch argues that human flourishing relies on us being able to accept two seemingly contradictory aspects of our natures: being both strong and weak. For us to thrive, Crouch argues, requires us to embrace both authority (I might prefer the term agency) and vulnerability. We tend to have various degrees of both of these in our lives, but Crouch says that the full life involves reckoning with each of them.[3] People should – and for the point of this discussion, let's say men and boys should – seek greater agency and greater vulnerability *at the same time*.

Some men will identify with and aspire to greater agency in places where they can make a difference with their creativity and leadership. Others will identify more closely with vulnerability. That might be their reality or their upbringing, but they will have a stronger sense of fragility, and dependence, and powerlessness.

Crouch makes the case that where people lack agency or authority and experience only vulnerability, they face exploitation and suffering. Where they have authority without vulnerability, they become the exploiters. Where either or both facets are missing, you have distortions of what it means to be human.

Ultimately, of course, we are all vulnerable and fragile creatures, subject to weakness and decay and death, even if we can build a life that looks secure and strong. Making peace with that reality is vital for mature and healthy living.

7. Ancient Wisdom for Modern Times

An old story for a new day

As I said at the beginning, I am someone who long ago was convinced by the story of Jesus, so it's no surprise that in a discussion about healthy masculinity I would be inclined to point to the first-century carpenter from Nazareth for some guidance. Irrespective of your beliefs and whether you accept the theological claims of Jesus, I think a consideration of his life and teaching would serve us well. What kind of picture of manhood do you get when you consider this person and what might that picture offer us today?

Andy Crouch's argument about strength and vulnerability comes directly from the life of Jesus and the apparent paradox inherent in his life of influence and enacted humility. Jesus' life is bookended with deeply human vulnerability. Born as a dependent infant and ending tortured and broken in crucifixion, in the years in between he exemplifies a model of authority that also identifies with vulnerability. At every point, Jesus is thoroughly human with all the vulnerability that entails. He needs to sleep and eat and rest. He gets puffed walking uphill, and when his skin is pierced, he bleeds. He feels sadness and pain and suffers like anyone else. Jesus weeps at the death of his friend and acknowledges when he is afraid.[4]

Yet Jesus' authority is writ large in the story. He has a magnetic personality that commands respect and awe. He displays authority when clearing the temple of money changers and those who had turned it into a market.[5] He commands demons and drives out sickness, and even the wind and the waves obey him.[6] The claims of his resurrection suggest that he has authority over death itself.

A radical life

The Graeco-Roman world of the first century that Jesus was born into was no place for the fainthearted. It was aggressive, patriarchal and brutal in the exercise of power. Highly stratified and hierarchical, it rewarded the strong and punished the weak.

It's hard for modern readers to comprehend the sheer brutality of that culture – equally evident in domestic settings as in spectacular public festivals of cruelty. The Graeco-Roman conception of the world was of an endless and unchangeable cycle, which meant only the high-born and powerful

7. Ancient Wisdom for Modern Times

benefited while the vast majority of people lacked any possibility of personal elevation. Remaining in your allotted station in life was not only right but morally necessary.

Against that background, Jesus' short life and even shorter public engagement exemplified the potency of a radically different way. In Jesus we see a restrained strength, composure and compassion. Throughout the Gospels he models a heart for the poor, the sick, the outcasts and rejects. Whether Jew or Gentile, male or female, adult or child, he exuded welcome and kindness. We see an example of openness to the pain of others and emotional engagement, not detachment, with those he encountered. Importantly, he sought to alleviate suffering and to bring life.

In a society that valued personal honour and self-aggrandisement, Jesus extolled a life of humility and putting others before himself. He taught that if you want to be truly great, you have to become a servant. Nobody was expecting that from the promised Messiah. But he made it very clear - in God's eyes, it's loving and serving others that has eternal value. He famously washed his disciples' feet in an enacted metaphor for how he expected his people to live and love. And then, according to the Gospel accounts, he lived that out in the most dramatic way imaginable, willingly going to a sacrificial death on a Roman cross in service of all humanity. It was all about giving rather than taking.

Jesus exemplified action and purpose. He worked hard in a physically demanding job, and he travelled the countryside and gave himself to the crowds in a manner than was exhausting. He fought against injustice and hypocrisy, and he engaged with his opponents by listening and offering incisive commentary and searching questions. He refused any kind of violence but was anything but passive. He went willingly into danger to fulfil his mission and courageously faced his enemies and his brutal fate so that others might live. There's 'no greater love' than that, as John's Gospel (and many of our war memorials) state. There has been no more influential life than his, and it's one we need have no misgivings about holding up as a model of vibrant masculinity.

Refusing to walk on by

One of the most famous stories Jesus ever told was the parable of the good Samaritan. It's found in Luke 10:25–37. It comes in the context of a legal debate between Jesus and a religious lawyer. After

7. Ancient Wisdom for Modern Times

a discussion about how to be right with God, the lawyer and Jesus agree that the Jewish Law says the key is to 'Love the Lord your God with all your heart, and with all your soul, and with all your strength and with all your mind'; and to 'Love your neighbour as yourself'. The lawyer, probably wanting to justify himself by limiting the list of those he is supposed to love, asks 'And who is my neighbour?'

In response, Jesus tells a story:

A man is travelling on the road from Jerusalem to Jericho, which is known as a dangerous route. He gets mugged. He's terribly beaten up, robbed, and left on the side of the road 'half dead'. A priest comes by. You could be forgiven for thinking that this is the rescue part, but no, the priest doesn't want to get caught up in whatever has gone on and deliberately crosses the road to pass by. Enter a Levite, or a minor priest, who does the same thing. Religious people don't get a good treatment in this story! Next comes a Samaritan. Here is the surprise. Samaritans were despised by the Jews. They were enemies. They were enemies to the extent that even if you were desperate, you might not want help from someone from that people group. In the normal run of things, you wouldn't be seen dead with them.

But in Jesus' story, it's the Samaritan who is the hero. He sees the man in distress and takes pity on him. He bathes and bandages his wounds, then takes him on his own donkey to an inn where he can take care of him. He then leaves money with the innkeeper to continue the restorative stay and promises to pay any further expenses when he returns.

Jesus asks, 'Which of these three do you think was a neighbour to the man who fell into the hands of robbers?'

The expert in the law replies, 'The one who had mercy on him.'

'Go and do likewise,' says Jesus.

This is a dramatic moment of public discussion and teaching. The crowds listening would have found this intensely confronting. In response to the question, 'Who is the neighbour that I am supposed to love?', Jesus blows away the limits we might want to impose on that category and calls for a radical love for all people, including our enemies. I can imagine people shuffling uncomfortably and staring at their feet as Jesus hit them with that one.

Parables function as a means of holding up a mirror, revealing even our worst impulses – the things we would rather were hidden. I've deliberately chosen a story here that applies to all people and not just men and boys, but it does

7. Ancient Wisdom for Modern Times

encapsulate qualities that, if embraced by men, would serve us all well. The action of the Samaritan illustrates a list of virtues I have been suggesting are important ones for men to cultivate: generosity of spirit to all people, kindness, compassion, empathy.

These virtues are combined with traits that, while not exclusively male, are ones that men, at their best, will exhibit. The Samaritan shows initiative and commitment to a cause. He carries through on his promise to help all the way to its conclusion. He shows courage in helping, despite the potential for social rejection, and confronts risk in order to do the right thing. He shows agency and strength and is a person of action not just words. He deploys everything he has in the service of someone in need. And 2,000 years later we are still talking about him!

There are lessons for young men to take from the parable and perhaps be inspired by. The first one: don't be the robbers! That's a start. Secondly, we are all unimpressed with the ones who selfishly move away from the injured man and leave him for dead. Too caught up in their own lives, they are not willing to put themselves out. Each of us senses, deep down, these priests are transgressing something profoundly important in our shared humanity. Thirdly, everyone recognises greatness in the act of sacrificial love – active love even for those who are not part of your tribe. It's a call to action that has inspired significant acts of similar sacrifice across the centuries. There is much to be gained by heeding this call to go out and act in the world for the good of others.

Jesus and women

Given that so much of our discussion on masculinity has been about the way in which men do or don't relate well to women, it's worth taking a moment to talk about Jesus and women. The Roman Empire in the first century was a man's world in every way. Women and girls were essentially chattel belonging to their fathers or brothers before being married off at very young ages to men who were usually several years older than them. In many cases women had no legal rights. Apart from aristocratic classes, women were rarely educated and so had very limited opportunities outside of the home and family. We know of some successful businesswomen in this period, but they were notable because they were so rare.

7. Ancient Wisdom for Modern Times

Into this environment came Jesus, who rode over the conventions of the time with an extraordinarily high view of women. Jesus was the only rabbi of his day that we know of with women disciples. He had female supporters and women who travelled with him. In Luke 8:1–3, Jesus was on the road with the twelve disciples plus Mary Magdalene, Joanna, Susanna and 'many others' (Mark 15:41). This was thoroughly scandalous for the time. In one famous incident at the house of Martha, we see a woman sitting at Jesus' feet to listen to him and be taught by him. In doing so, she had adopted the place of learning that was traditionally set aside for the (male) disciples of prominent teachers.

In Jesus' famous parables, women often feature as the heroes of the story. Every historical Jesus scholar notes the unusually high place given to women in his story.

Jesus offers a robust affirmation of the dignity and full humanity of women – something for men to aspire to today. Dorothy Sayers, the English crime writer and poet, once described Jesus' interaction with women like this:

> Perhaps it is no wonder that the women were first at the Cradle and last at the Cross. They had never known a man like this Man – there never has been such another. A prophet and teacher who

never nagged at them, never flattered or coaxed or patronised; who never made arch jokes about them, never treated them either as 'The women, God help us!' or 'The ladies, God bless them!'; who rebuked without querulousness and praised without condescension; who took their questions and arguments seriously; who never mapped out their sphere for them, never urged them to be feminine or jeered at them for being female; who had no axe to grind and no uneasy male dignity to defend; who took them as he found them and was completely unself-conscious.[7]

The Jesus we find from a close reading of the Gospels offers an intriguing, sometimes unsettling, but always inspiring portrait of a man worth listening to and emulating.

A modern code?

In June 2023, after a series of claims of sexual misconduct by men in federal parliament, my friend and colleague Justine Toh wrote a piece in *The Sydney Morning Herald* with a call to 'Make chivalry great again'. It was a largely tongue-in-cheek attempt to address this alleged behaviour. But it made a serious point too. Justine acknowledged that chivalry seems outdated, condescending and benevolently sexist in that it suggests that helpless women are in need of the protection of men: "For liberated moderns, chivalry reinforces rigid and retrograde gender roles: think brave knights and swooning damsels in distress, or excessive, flowery displays of courtly honour that underline female helplessness."[8]

Chivalry as it existed as a social, moral and religious code for medieval knights might sit awkwardly with today's sensibilities, but Justine urged us to consider a 21st-century reboot of the chivalry code: one that encourages men to recognise that they share the world with multiple others, urges men to be sensitive to inequality and power imbalances, and reminds all of us that humility and respect are vital for healthy social relations.

That kind of reimagined code could, as Andy Crouch urges, help men to balance strength and vulnerability, think about not only how they treat women but everyone else, and be fierce in battling on behalf of others while maintaining humility and restraint. Importantly, it could include knowing how and when to accept help yourself, recognising that no person is an island and all are vulnerable at various points.

Justine Toh's call for a reimagining of something akin to chivalry chimes with Christine Emba's essay in *The Washington Post* on helping men navigate their way out of a modern wilderness. Emba commends a fresh look at masculinity that recognises its distinctive traits and powerful narratives – strength, self-mastery, adventure, risk-taking, the instinct to protect and provide – carefully directed towards 'pro-social' ends.[9]

In his book *The Good Life: What Makes a Life Worth Living?*, social researcher Hugh Mackay, who has spent decades listening to Australians talk about their lives, concluded with this striking observation: 'Nobody can promise you that a life lived for others will bring you a deep sense of satisfaction, but it's certain that nothing else will.'[10]

Nothing else will do it! Not fame, not success, not wealth, not pleasure. In an ultimate sense, none of these will satisfy deep down. We need something more, and according to the wisdom of Jesus via the wisdom of Hugh Mackay(!), meaning and satisfaction is found only in an orientation of the heart that is outwards, towards others and their benefit. Mackay says we need a good sense of self so that we will resist exploitation and mistreatment, and then be in a better position to help others – which he says everyone can do, even in small ways.

We all need to hear that message of the full life coming from self-giving rather than

7. Ancient Wisdom for Modern Times

taking. If boys and men could be provided with convincing reasons to embrace it, the difference could be amazing. The 'manosphere', the 'incel' phenomenon, the Andrew Tates of the world show that some are responding to the contemporary challenge for males in insidious and dangerous ways. A backlash to male anguish that is retrograde, limiting and harmful is a genuine threat.

A viable alternative is both imaginable and possible. But it won't just happen. Left to their own devices, without the nurture of strong community focused on positive outcomes, young men tend to drift into destructive patterns of behaviour.

In the opening chapter I mentioned academic David Hastie, and his traumatic experiences at the school we both attended. Hastie has become a big believer in developing good systems that form protective layers around vulnerable kids and help to prevent abusive environments. He also advocates an 'ethos of love and care' from effective and purposeful leaders.

Reflecting on his childhood, he says:

> The boarding school could have been a place where young men were led and guided into paths of reciprocity, honour, and courage, given the right programmes and peer structures. Instead we were led into paths of selfishness and brutality, indignity and shame.

But those experiences did not, in the end, define who David Hastie would become. He fell into teaching in his early 20s while doing a PhD and came to love it. He flourished as a teacher with the opportunity to offer something so different from what he experienced as a student:

> I came to believe, and to observe, that the role of positive spiritual formation in schools, and a dedicated staff motivated by a credo of love and divinely endowed dignity of the child, was one pathway to building a schooling that was kinder to both the child and broader society. I embraced this approach, and later became a theorist and a public apologist of these approaches as an education academic. However, I have also worked to build better teacher-training models in Australian education more generally, including a focus on hard-to-staff regional schools. It has been healing to know that I can make that difference.

His is a good story of gaining a sense of healing by becoming an agent of positive change. Hastie shares with me a belief that building healthy cultures for young men is possible and also vital.

> I managed over time to climb out of that dark place, thank God. And perhaps those experiences led to the stronger self I am today. But perhaps not. I cannot change the past. But we can build a better world.

7. Ancient Wisdom for Modern Times

In the time I have reflected on this topic, I have become even more convinced that boys and men are struggling, and their plight is in need of attention. My sense is that efforts to address that plight will need at least four elements: Firstly, they will need to be intentional and carefully thought through at every level of young men's development. Parents of boys need to be made aware of the challenges that await their sons and be consciously addressing these challenges from an early age. Schools need to consider programs that address areas of obvious need for boys at each stage of their development - ones that are supportive and focused. They need to partner with families and community groups to foster initiatives that, for example, develop emotional literacy, expression and intelligence.

Secondly, the posture needs to be positive. We need to be appealing to the better natures of our boys and men and not giving the impression that there is something inherently negative about being a male. We need to be focused on cultivating the best traits that boys have and directing them in productive and life-giving directions.

Thirdly, it must be modelled. We need to address the challenges of boys as a community, engaging with sports clubs, schools, volunteering organisations and faith communities. As we've heard from all the experts, boys need examples they can follow and lives they can mirror that are attractive, compelling and liveable. Some boys and men have never had anything like that in their lives. Those of us who have, carry an extra responsibility to be that figure for someone else. As we have seen, not only fathers but father figures play potentially enormous roles. As do those who are a little older than you who can pass on wisdom hewn from experience.

Finally, in addressing some of the challenges males face – confusion about roles, wounds from childhood, a rapidly changing world where labour markets now skew towards traditionally female skills, and where family roles have rapidly shifted – I have appealed to a broad sense of who men can be today and what being a male might look like. At the same time, I've suggested that an orientation of the heart towards love and service of the other is the key to the fullest life possible. This is something that doesn't come naturally to many of us, but boys in particular might need convincing of the benefit of deploying whatever strength they possess in the service of others and not themselves. But if captivated by that vision, even males who have only ever glimpsed that truth from afar, or were shown precious little by way of example in their growing up, can not only offer something invaluable to those looking up to them, but find a pathway to a new and fulfilling life themselves.

Re:CONSIDERING

NOTES

1. THE DAMAGE DONE

[1] Tim Winton, interview, 'Hope is violent' [podcast], *Life & Faith*, Centre for Public Christianity, 29 March 2018, accessed 2 April 2024, italics added, https://www.publicchristianity.org/hope-is-violent/

2. WE HAVE A PROBLEM

[1] Australia's National Research Organisation for Women's Safety, 'Violence against women: accurate use of key statistics' [PDF 514KB], *ANROWS Insights* (ANROWS, Sydney NSW, May 2018), accessed 2 April 2024, https://www.anrows.org.au/resources/fact-sheet-violence-against-women-accurate-use-of-key-statistics/

[2] 'STOP Kit', *White Ribbon Australia*, 2024, accessed 2 April 2024, https://www.whiteribbon.org.au/stop-kit/

[3] Shane Wright, 'When women earn more than their male partners, domestic violence risk goes up 35 per cent', *The Sydney Morning Herald*, 30 March 2021,

accessed 13 March 2024, https://www.smh.com.au/politics/federal/when-women-earn-more-than-their-male-partners-domestic-violence-risk-goes-up-35-per-cent-20210329-p57ewb.html

[4] Louise Milligan (producer), 'Boys club: private school privilege and a culture of cover up', *Four Corners*, ABC News, 17 February 2020, accessed 2 April 2024, https://www.youtube.com/watch?v=PyxPM-g6U2g&ab_channel=ABCNewsIn-depth

[5] Ibid.

[6] 'Pornography and harm to children and young people symposium', *Collective Shout*, 9 February 2016, accessed 2 April 2024, https://www.collectiveshout.org/media_release_phk

[7] M.J. Fleming, S. Greentree, D. Cocotti-Muller, K.A. Elias and S. Morrison, 'Safety in cyberspace: adolescents' safety and exposure online' (*Youth and Society*, vol. 38, no. 2, 2006), pp. 135–54, http://www.itstimewetalked.com.au/parents/things-to-know-about-porn-for-parents/

[8] Department of Education, Training and Youth Affairs, 'The education of boys' [PDF 185KB], Submission to the House of Representatives Standing Committee on Employment, Education and Workplace Relations, 2000.

[9] Steve Biddulph, *The New Manhood: Love, Freedom, Spirit and the New Masculinity* (Simon & Shuster, New York, 2019), p. 6.

[10] Warren Farrell and John Gray, *The Boy Crisis: Why Our Boys Are Struggling and What Can Be Done about It* (BenBella Books, Dallas TX, 2019), p. 34.

[11] Ibid., p. 34

[12] Marleen De Belle, 'The emergence of sex differences in personality traits in early adolescence: a cross-sectional, cross-cultural study' (*Journal of Personality and Social Psychology*, vol. 108, no. 1, 2015), pp. 171–185, accessed 12 March 2024, https://www.ncbi.nlm.nih.gov/pmc/articles/PMC4327943/

[13] Thomas B. Edsall, 'It's become increasingly hard for them to feel good about themselves', *The New York Times*, 22 September 2021, accessed 12 March 2024, https://www.nytimes.com/2021/09/22/opinion/economy-education-women-men.html?referringSource=articleShare

[14] Hannah Rosin, 'The end of men', *The Atlantic*, 8 June 2010, accessed 12 March 2024, https://www.theatlantic.com/magazine/archive/2010/07/the-end-of-men/308135/

[15] Ibid.

[16] Pete Shmigel, 'Australia's "bloke blindspot" – we keep overlooking the people most at risk of suicide', *The Sydney Morning Herald*, 19 November 2020, accessed 12 March 2024, https://www.smh.com.au/national/australia-s-bloke-blindspot-we-keep-overlooking-the-people-most-at-risk-of-suicide-20201119-p56fyf.html

[17] Tim Lobstein, Hannah Brinsden and Margot Neveux, 'World obesity atlas 2022', *World Obesity*, 2022, accessed 2 April 2024, https://www.worldobesity.org/resources/resource-library/world-obesity-atlas-2022

[18] Andrology Australia: Australian Centre of Excellence in Male Reproductive Health, 'The current state of male health in Australia' [PDF650KB], July 2018, accessed 12 March 2024, https://consultations.health.gov.au/population-health-and-sport-division-1/online-consultation-for-the-national-mens-health-s/supporting_documents/Evidence%20Review%20%20Current%20state%20of%20male%20health%20in%20Australia.PDF

[19] See Martha Nussbaum's chapter in James L. Harmon, *Take My Advice: Letter to the Next Generation from People Who Know a Thing or Two* (Simon & Shuster, New York, 2010).

[20] Richard Reeves, *Of Boys and Men: Why the Modern Male Is Struggling, Why It Matters and What to Do about It* (Swift Press, United Kingdom, 2023), p. 126.

[21] William R. Fuller, 'The military masculine: storytelling and role-playing in Phil Klay's stories of war', *Inquiries*, vol. 11, no. 4, 2019), p. 1/1, accessed 13 March 2024, http://www.inquiriesjournal.com/articles/1762/the-military-masculine-storytelling-and-role-playing-in-phil-klays-stories-of-war

3. MODELS OF MASCULINITY

[1] Mark Moss, *The Media and Models of Masculinity* (Lexington Books, UK, 2011), preface.

[2] Ibid., p. 2.

[3] Ibid., p. 10.

[4] Ibid., p. 5.

[5] Ibid., p. 9.

[6] Dan Kindlon and Michael Thompson, *Raising Cain: Protecting the Emotional Life of Boys* (Ballantine Books, New York, 2000), p. 15.

[7] Susan Faludi, *Stiffed: The Betrayal of the American Man* (William Morrow and Company, New York, 1999), pp. 38–39.

[8] Ruth Whippman, 'What we are not teaching boys about being human', *The New York Times*, 6 August 2021, p. 2.

[9] Ibid., p. 2.

[10] Michael Black, 'The boys are not all right', *The New York Times*, 21 February 2018.

[11] Ibid.

[12] Manohla Dargis, 'Men are in trouble and Hollywood wants to help', *The New York Times*, 19 December 2019, accessed 31 January 2024, https://www.nytimes.com/2019/12/19/movies/men-in-trouble.html

[13] Moss, *The Media and Models of Masculinity*, p. 7.

[14] William S. Pollack, with Todd Shuster, *Real Boys' Voices* (New York: Random House, 2000), p. xix.

[15] Ibid., p. xxv.

[16] Jesuit Social Services, *The Men's Project*, Jesuit Social Services website, 2023, accessed 15 November 2021, https://jss.org.au/what-we-do/the-mens-project/

4. MEN, MAYHEM AND MUTUAL BENEFIT

[1] Jasmeet Sidhu, 'How to buy a daughter: choosing the sex of your baby has become a multimillion-dollar industry', *Slate Magazine*, 14 September 2012, accessed 22 December 2022, https://slate.com/technology/2012/09/sex-selection-in-babies-through-pgd-americans-are-paying-to-have-daughters-rather-than-sons.html

[2] Farrell & Gray, *The Boy Crisis*, p. 79.

[3] Reeves, *Of Boys and Men*, p. 132.

[4] Ibid., p. 132.

[5] Ibid., p. 132.

[6] Ibid., p. 110.

[7] Ibid., p 134.

[8] Faludi, *Stiffed*, pp. 24–28.

[9] Ibid., p. 43

[10] Kevin Donnelly, 'Why boys are falling behind at school', *The Sydney Morning Herald*, 2 November

2022, accessed 23 December 2022, https://www.smh.com.au/education/why-boys-are-falling-behind-at-school-20221101-p5burn.html

[11] Jordan Baker, 'Boys falling far behind girls in HSC and at university', *The Sydney Morning Herald*, 14 June 2022, accessed 23 December 2022, https://www.smh.com.au/national/nsw/boys-falling-far-behind-girls-in-hsc-and-at-university-20220607-p5arsk.html

[12] Donnelly, 'Why boys are falling behind at school'.

[13] Andrew FitzSimons, phone interview, 17 December 2022.

[14] Quoted in Reeves, *Of Boys and Men*, p. 141.

[15] Faludi, *Stiffed*, pp. 9, 10.

[16] Ibid., p. 11.

[17] Ibid., p. 13.

[18] Farrell & Gray, *The Boy Crisis*, p. 77.

[19] Reeves, *Of Boys and Men*, p. 146.

[20] Shanti Das, 'Inside the violent, misogynistic world of TikTok's new star, Andrew Tate', *The Guardian*, 7 August 2022, accessed 14 March 2024, https://www.theguardian.com/technology/2022/aug/06/andrew-tate-violent-misogynistic-world-of-tiktok-new-star

[21] James Purtoll, 'Booted from Facebook and Instagram, Andrew Tate is now being scrubbed from TikTok. Is this the end for his misogyny?', *ABC News*, 22 August 2022, accessed 22 February 2023, https://

www.abc.net.au/news/2022-08-22/misogynist-influencer-andrew-tate-is-being-scrubbed-from-tiktok/101356652

[22] Caitlin Flanagan, 'In praise of heroic masculinity', *The Atlantic*, 30 August 2023.

[23] Arthur Schlesinger Jr., 'The crisis of American masculinity', *Esquire*, 1 November 1958.

[24] Faludi, *Stiffed*, p. 595.

5. SIGNS OF LIFE

[1] Andrew McUtchen, interview, 'The father hood', *Life & Faith* podcast, Centre for Public Christianity, 2 September 2021, https://www.publicchristianity.org/the-father-hood/

[2] Reeves, *Of Boys and Men*, p. 200.

[3] Biddulph, *The New Manhood*, p. 186.

[4] Mary Ward, 'Men go to the Pub, but don't know each other', *The Sydney Morning Herald*, 30 October 2022, accessed 14 March 2024, https://www.smh.com.au/national/nsw/men-go-to-the-pub-but-don-t-know-each-other-20221026-p5bt4j.html

[5] Matt Andrews, interview with author.

[6] National Public Radio, 'The 3 scariest words a boy can hear', *All Things Considered*, NPR website, 14 July 2014, accessed 2 April 2024, https://www.npr.org/2014/07/14/330183987/the-3-scariest-words-a-boy-can-hear

[7] Joe Ehrmann, 'Be a man' [video], *TEDx talk*, YouTube, Baltimore, 2013, accessed 24 February 2023, https://www.youtube.com/watch?v=jVI1Xutc_Ws&ab_channel=TEDxTalks

[8] William Pollack, *Real Boys: Rescuing Our Sons from the Myths of Boyhood* (Henry Holt and Company, New York, 1999), p. 398.

[9] Kindlon & Thompson, *Raising Cain*, p. 7.

[10] 'About Collective Shout', *Collective Shout*, 2024, accessed 2 April 2024, https://www.collectiveshout.org/about

[11] Daniel Principe, interview with author.

[12] Anthony Segaert, 'Daniel wishes the rest of the world could witness what he sees in Australian high schools', *The Sydney Morning Herald*, 7 July 2023, accessed 13 July 2023, https://www.smh.com.au/national/nsw/daniel-wishes-the-rest-of-the-world-could-witness-what-he-sees-in-australia-s-high-schools-20230424-p5d2s0.html

6. REMEDIES

[1] Biddulph, *The New Manhood*.

[2] David Gilmore, cited in Christine Emba, 'Men are lost. Here's a map out of the wilderness', *The Washington Post*, 10 July 2023, accessed 24 August 2023, https://www.washingtonpost.com/opinions/2023/07/10/christine-emba-masculinity-new-model/

[3] Ehrmann, 'Be a man'.

[4] Emily Badger, Claire Cain Miller, Adam Pearce and Kevin Quealy, 'Extensive data shows punishing reach of racism for black boys', *The New York Times*, 19 March 2018, accessed 14 March 2024, https://www.nytimes.com/interactive/2018/03/19/upshot/race-class-white-and-black-men.html

[5] Bruce Robinson, interview with author.

[6] Andrew FitzSimons, interview with author.

[7] Timothy Wright, interview with author.

[8] See Richard Rohr, *Adam's Return: The Five Promises of Male Initiation* (The Crossroad Publishing Company, New York, 2004).

[9] Daniel Principe, interview with author.

[10] Reeves, *Of Boys and Men*, p. 181.

[11] Timothy Wright, interview with author.

7. ANCIENT WISDOM FOR MODERN TIMES

[1] Timothy Wright, interview with author.

[2] Christine Emba, 'Consent is not enough. We need a new sexual ethic', *The Washington Post*, 17 March 2022, accessed 14 March 2024, https://www.washingtonpost.com/opinions/2022/03/17/sex-ethics-rethinking-consent-culture/

[3] See Andy Crouch, *Strong and Weak: Embracing a*

Life of Love, Risk and True Flourishing (InterVarsity Press, Westmont IL, 2016).

[4] Noah Van Niel, 'Manly virtues: can masculinity be good?', *Plough Quarterly*, 22 January 2021, pp. 92–98.

[5] Matthew 21:12 17; John 2:13–22.

[6] Matthew 8:28–34; Luke 17:11–19 and Mark 5:21–43; Matthew 8:23–27.

[7] Dorothy L. Sayers, 'The human-not-quite human' [essay], in *Are Women Human? Astute and Witty Essays on the Role of Women in Society* (Eerdmans, Grand Rapids, 2005), p. 68.

[8] Justine Toh, 'Oh men behave! We need to make chivalry great again', *The Sydney Morning Herald*, 26 June 2023, accessed 14 March 2024, https://www.smh.com.au/lifestyle/life-and-relationships/oh-behave-we-need-to-make-chivalry-great-again-amen-20230626-p5djfl.html

[9] Emba, 'Men are lost'.

[10] Hugh McKay, *The Good Life: What Makes a Life Worth Living?* (Pan Macmillan, Sydney, 2013), p. 254.

Re:CONSIDERING

ALSO AVAILABLE

Scan this code for more information

Who's in favour of compassion?

Pretty much everybody, actually.

Left or right, religious or not, nobody seems to have a bad word to say about compassion.

So why do we have so much trouble addressing the conflict, inequality, and suffering in our world?

Ranging from the streets of St Kilda to the slums of Delhi, from Plato to Nietzsche, the Dalai Lama to Peter Singer, and from *Seinfeld* to the Good Samaritan, Tim Costello appeals to our common humanity – and takes an unflinching look at how costly compassion can be.

Re:CONSIDERING

ALSO AVAILABLE

Scan this code for more information

Are you an achievement addict?

It's hard not to be one given our collective obsession with success.

Students fear that the ATAR will sum up not just their schooling career, but also their individual worth. Australians aren't just mad for sporting victory – skyrocketing house prices show we're equally hooked on owning property. Then there are the furious work habits of Silicon Valley CEOs, violin prodigies, and tiger mums.

Why do we constantly strive for our significance – and could you quit the habit if you tried?

Re:CONSIDERING

ALSO AVAILABLE

Scan this code for more information

Pandemic, supervolcano, late capitalism, transhumanism, populism, cancel culture, the post-antibiotic age, the gig economy, the surveillance state, the cascading effects of climate change …

Whatever the specifics, do you feel like things have gone off the rails – or are just about to?

If you've read the news, watched a zombie movie, or gotten into an argument on Twitter lately, the answer is probably yes.

And you're not alone.

What makes us such apocaholics?

What's so appealing about Armageddon? What are the pleasures – and also the perils – of our pessimism?

Re:CONSIDERING

ALSO AVAILABLE

Scan this code for more information

What were you thinking?

We all feel entitled to our opinion. Whether it be our take on politics, vaccines, parenting, or the value of religion, everybody wants to have their say - and everybody loves to be right.

But do we know what it means to think well?

Covering 'idiot brain', lobotomies, the difference between certainty and confidence, the nature of facts, and the virtue of intellectual hospitality, Mark Stephens invites you to consider not just what you think but how and why you think.

Do we think only for ourselves, or also for the good of others?